ASTRONOMY
LAB
for Kids

ASTRONOMY
LAB
for Kids

MICHELLE NICHOLS, M.Ed.

52 Family-Friendly Activities

QUARRY

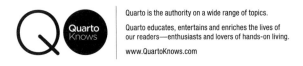

Quarto is the authority on a wide range of topics.

Quarto educates, entertains and enriches the lives of our readers—enthusiasts and lovers of hands-on living.

www.QuartoKnows.com

First published in the United States of America in 2016 by

Quarry Books, an imprint of

Quarto Publishing Group USA Inc.

100 Cummings Center

Suite 406-L

Beverly, Massachusetts 01915-6101

Telephone: (978) 282-9590

Fax: (978) 283-2742

QuartoKnows.com

Visit our blogs at QuartoKnows.com

10 9 8 7 6 5 4 3 2 1

ISBN: 978-1-63159-134-1

Digital edition published in 2016

eISBN: 978-1-63159-198-3

Library of Congress Cataloging-in-Publication Data available

Design: Marie-Anne Verougstraete

Page Layout: Marie-Anne Verougstraete

Photography: David Miller, Miller Visual

Printed in China

I would like to dedicate this book to the following people:

- First and foremost, my parents, who always encouraged me to reach for the stars in everything I have ever done

- My family and friends, who never, ever said, "No, you shouldn't do that," and especially my brother Mark who is as geeked-out about science as I am

- And last, but never least, my husband, Brian, who has been my number-one fan

Thank you, all. You have inspired me and encouraged me more than you will ever know.

Unit 1
Observing

Unit 2
Scope It Out!

Unit 3
Size and Scale

Unit 4
Light, Motion, Gravity

Unit 5
Exploring Our Solar System

Unit 6
Seeing Stars

Introduction

As far back as I can remember, I have observed the sky. One of my earliest memories is of riding in the back of my parents' car, looking out the window, and exclaiming, "URFO, URFO!" URFO was my five-year-old way of pointing out something I couldn't identify . . . something flashing, something moving against a background of twinkly things that weren't flashing or moving as quickly. It also may very well have been a conglomeration of seeing airplanes and watching *Close Encounters of the Third Kind* a few too many times. No matter. If there was something flying in the sky that I couldn't identify, it was a UFO—or, rather, a URFO. More importantly, searching for these things got me in the habit of looking up.

The night sky of my hometown was amazing. Back then, it was still dark enough that we could see the Milky Way from our backyard. Many a summer Saturday night was spent popping popcorn, watching the sky, and pointing our small telescope at whatever we could find. I even had a homemade observing kit containing my handwritten notebook, my binoculars, my constellation finder wheel, and my astronomy guide. In my notebook, I drew the stars of the Big Dipper. I learned how to find objects in the sky. I sketched the Moon. One image, though, is seared into my memory: the very first time I ever saw Saturn through our telescope. It was amazing! I could see the rings! Saturn became more than just a picture on television or in a book. It became *a place, a world* to observe and explore. Astronomy became very real for me from then onward. I wanted to learn more.

This drive to learn and know still inspires me today to help connect children and adults to the sky above us. As a museum educator for more than twenty years, my primary job has been to help people figure out what's out there and how it all works. I want everyone to understand that no expensive equipment is required to begin to investigate the world—and worlds—around us. The Universe is an amazing place to explore. Just bring your curiosity and your wonder . . . and don't forget to look up!

The Hubble Space Telescope captured light from about two million stars in the cluster called Omega Centauri.
Credit: NASA, ESA, and the Hubble Heritage Team (STScI/AURA)

Overview

A variety of activities is contained in this book. Many can be done in one sitting, but others require observations over a few hours, a few days, or even a few months, depending on what you are investigating. You probably have many of the materials needed around your house already, and others that you may not have are simple to obtain. I also recommend that you start keeping a science journal or notebook to record your observations, results, questions, comments, and drawings. This will help you, especially for those activities that take longer periods of time to complete or that require several sessions.

Each lab contains an easy-to-understand explanation of the vocabulary and ideas you will explore, and each contains the following sections:

→ **Time** shows you approximately how long it will take to complete all the steps.

→ **Materials** lists all the items you'll need to conduct each lab.

→ **Safety Tips and Setup Hints** gives you common-sense guidelines to make your investigations as safe and enjoyable as possible and highlights some steps to do in advance, if needed.

→ **Instructions** takes you step by step through a lab.

→ **The Science Behind the Fun** offers digestible explanations for each lab.

→ **Creative Enrichment** gives you variations or ideas for taking the project a step or two further.

Hopefully, you'll be inspired to come up with some additional ideas of your own.

This book contains activities that are tried, true, and tested, and they will help you begin to make sense of the Sun, Moon, planets, and stars. Several of the tools created for some of the earlier activities will be used in later ones. One thing this book is not, however, is an encyclopedia of everything you ever wanted to know about astronomy. That would be too much for one book! More Resources (see page 140) gives you some suggestions for taking advantage of stellar astronomy resources online and in your community to extend your explorations even further.

Parents, this book is as much for you as it is for your children. Help them with concepts and vocabulary, and assist with the activities where you can. Hopefully, everyone will learn something new.

Please keep in mind throughout your investigations that science is more than just the results of an experiment or activity. Science is messy and fun. Scientists ask questions, such as *why, how, what, where, and when*—as we all do! Science is about answering questions and then asking a hundred more. Science is not just about finding the "right" answer; scientists learn just as much from their failures as their successes. Science is wonder and science is discovery; so together, let's wonder about and discover more about our place in the Universe!

Science Journal

Scientists keep personal notebooks to document and detail background research, experiments, interesting results, thoughts, ideas, and questions. Some keep paper notebooks and others keep electronic ones. Why do they do this? Shouldn't they be spending their time doing experiments?

While experiments are important to many scientists, one of the most important skills for a scientist to practice is the ability to communicate ideas to an audience. A fantastic experiment with wonderful results means nothing if you can't explain to someone else what happened. There are several reasons for honing these skills. First, a scientist wants others to know the results of an experiment or the progress that has been made in researching something new. Secondly, a scientist wants others to be able to *replicate* the same experiment that was performed, meaning another person or team should be able to follow the experiment instructions to repeat them to confirm (or disprove!) the results. Thirdly, science is usually done by teams of men and women working together, not by individuals working completely alone. It is important for the team members to communicate well with one another so everyone can keep up with what everyone else is doing. Finally, some experiments may take a very long time to complete, and it would be extremely difficult to remember what happened months or years earlier if notes weren't kept all along the way.

Your family can practice keeping your own individual science notebooks as you do the activities in this book. Here is a sample format you may want to follow.

Name: your name

Date: today's date

What I Will Do: a quick summary of the lab you are going to do, in your own words

My Questions: questions you have about the activity before you start

My Materials: the materials you plan to use in the lab

My Observations: observations you make during the lab; what you see, hear, touch

My Data: the information, or data, you collect during the lab; don't forget to label your units—weights, lengths, times, and so on.

My Reflections: your feelings about how you think the lab went, what you think the lab results mean, and any answers to your questions you have found

My Concerns: any issues or problems you encountered, plus any solutions you came up with

Is it okay to include artwork if you would rather draw than write? Of course it is! Use any format you are comfortable with that helps you keep track of what you are doing. Remember, there is no single "correct" format. Use what works best for you.

After you've completed one of the activities in this book, think of other ways you could address the same ideas. Try some of the enrichment activities or invent a new way to do the same lab. How can what you have learned be applied to the world around you? Write down your thoughts in your notebook so you can come back to them in the future.

Observing

Often in school, we are told to "observe something." Observe this experiment. Observe what happens when a liquid is added to a powder. But what does it *mean* to observe? Am I just supposed to watch something happen? How do I know what to look for?

The skill of observation involves much more than just pointing your eyes in the direction of something. Observing is an *active* experience utilizing your senses of touch, smell, sight, taste,

and hearing. Observing also involves using instruments to extend your senses and recording information from your observations.

The following activities will get your senses rolling—from observing angles in the sky, directions, and apparent motions of the Sun, to observations that can tell you about twinkling stars, the color of the Sun, and the phases of the Moon. Let's start practicing our skills of observation by using our senses and simple materials.

This view of the Full Moon was taken by NASA's *Clementine* spacecraft in 1994.
Credit: NASA/Goddard Space Flight Center Scientific Visualization Studio

LAB 01

Making Observations

Time
10 minutes

Materials

- Paper lunch bag, pillowcase, reusable grocery bag, or any other opaque bag
- Small items from around the house with interesting textures, shapes, or materials
- Your science notebook
- Pencil

Safety Tips and Setup Hints

- The more interesting items you choose for this lab, the better! However, **be very careful that your items do not contain sharp edges, pointy pieces, or have materials that are dangerous to touch, smell, or handle**. Do not choose objects that are especially warm or cold.

How do I observe if I can't see? Use your other senses!

Instructions

Step 1: Choose who will be the Leader and who will be the Observer.

Step 2: Leader, place one item in the bag without the Observer seeing what you have selected.

Observer, use your senses of touch, smell, and hearing as you carefully reach into the bag and touch the item, pick it up, carefully shake it, smell it, but do not look into the bag at all. If you need to pull the item out of the bag to make your observations, close your eyes so you do not see it. (Fig. 1)

Step 3: Observer, tell the Leader what you notice about the item. What does it feel like? What is it made of? Is it heavy or light? Does it have an odor? Is it smooth or rough? Is it made of metal, wood, plastic, fabric, or more than one material? How big is it? Does it remind you of something else? Is it made of parts or is it one piece? Does it make a sound when you move or shake it? Does it feel warm or cool? As you make your various observations, say them aloud.

Leader, as the Observer makes his or her observations, write them in your science notebook. (Fig. 2)

Step 4: Observer, once you have made all your initial observations, use your sense of sight to look at the object. What color is it? Is it shiny or dull? Is it transparent, translucent, or opaque?

Leader, record the observations made by the Observer. Finally, draw sketches of the object from the top or bottom, from the side, or from close-up or far away. (Fig. 3) ✦

The Science Behind the Fun

Did you notice the goal of this lab is not to try to guess what the item in the bag actually is? You could do that, if you wanted to, but the main goal was to involve *all* your senses to determine different scientific characteristics of an object, such as its length, width, height, weight, what it is made of, its sounds, and smells, how it moves (or doesn't move), and more. Only after figuring out everything you could without looking at it could you actually use your sense of sight to fill in the blanks this sense could tell you, such as the color of an object or whether it was shiny. Sketching an object is also a very important scientific step, as seeing something from different viewpoints can tell you about how the object works, what its pieces do, or how it changes over time. Making complete observations with as many details as possible can tell you a lot about an object, and making good observations is a very important part of science—especially astronomy!

Creative Enrichment

Take your notebook and a pencil into a park, field, or forest. Find a comfortable spot where you can sit for a while. Make observations of what you see, hear, smell, and touch. Sketch the scene in front of you and to your right or left. Try to go to the same location in summer, fall, winter, and spring and repeat your observations. How does that place change over time? Record all your observations in your notebook.

Take your notebook and a pencil outside at night. Look at the Moon or the stars. Make observations of what you see, but also don't forget to observe the scene around you. Record as many details as you can. Go out a few days, weeks, or months later and repeat your observations as often as you can. Is the sky starting to become a little more familiar to you?

Fig. 1: Place an object in the bag.

Fig. 2: Is the object big? Small? Heavy? Light? Rough? Smooth?

Fig. 3: Use your sense of sight to make your observations complete. Light? Rough? Smooth?

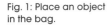

Angles in Your Hands

Time
5 minutes

Materials
• Your hands

Safety Tips and Setup Hints
• To find angles properly, make sure your arm is fully stretched out. Keep your elbow and your arm straight.

How far apart are objects in the sky? Use your simplest—and best!—tools to figure it out: your hands!

Instructions

Step 1: Stretch out your arm and stick out only your pinky (smallest) finger. The rest of your fingers should be closed. Find something off in the distance to compare to the size of the end of your pinky finger. Look down your arm at your pinky. The angle made by one side of your pinky finger to the other is one degree. If you are looking at something in the distance and it exactly matches the size of just the end of your outstretched pinky, we can say that object is one degree wide or tall. (Fig. 1)

Step 2: Stretch out your thumb. The angle made by one side of your thumb to the other is two degrees, so something off in the distance that is the same size as the end of your thumb is two degrees wide or tall. (Fig. 2)

Step 3: Stretch out your arm and make a closed fist. Hold your fist straight outward. The angle from the bottom of your pinky finger to the top of your index finger is about ten degrees. The angles made by your pinky (one degree), thumb (two degrees), and closed fist (ten degrees) are the angles you probably will use most often when observing the sky. (Fig. 3)

Fig. 1: The width of one pinky equals one degree.

Fig. 2: The width of one thumb equals two degrees.

Step 4: There are a few other angles you might find useful. Stretch out your middle three fingers so those fingers touch. The angle from one edge of your index finger to the outer edge of your ring finger is about five degrees. Next, stretch out your hand so your index finger and pinky finger are angled outward. The angle between your two fingers is about fifteen degrees. Finally, stretch out your hand so your pinky finger and thumb are angled outward. The angle between your thumb and pinky is about twenty-five degrees.

Step 5: Go outside to a place where you can see at least part of the horizon in the distance and the sky up over your head. Make a fist and stretch it out so the bottom of your fist meets the horizon. From the bottom of your fist to the top is equal to ten degrees. If you put one fist on top of the other all the way up to the top of the sky, how many fists do you need to reach directly above your head? It should be nine. Nine fists of ten degrees each equal ninety degrees. This point straight up in the sky has a special name. It is called the "zenith." The point opposite the zenith, straight down to the ground directly under your feet, is called the "nadir." The sky looks like a bowl up over your head down to the horizon on the ground. That much sky is half of a circle, or 180 degrees. ◆

Fig. 3: The height of one fist equals ten degrees.

The Science Behind the Fun

Draw a circle. If you draw a line down the middle of the circle from top to bottom, you now have divided the circle into two equal pieces. If you add a line across the middle going from the left side of the circle to the right side, you now have four equal pieces. Another way to divide the circle is to draw 180 lines so you end up with 360 little pie shapes that are all the same size. Each rounded edge along the edge of the circle is equal to 1 degree. The length of ten of those small rounded edges put together is equal to ten degrees of distance. One-half of a circle is 180 degrees, and one full circle equals 360 degrees.

Scientists use degrees to indicate how far apart objects appear in the sky. In many cases, though, one degree is still too large to describe how far apart objects are. For those small angles, they also divide each degree into even smaller pieces.

Creative Enrichment

Have you ever noticed how large the Moon appears to be when it is close to the horizon? Compare the size of the Moon to the width of your pinky (smallest) finger or your thumb when the Moon is close to the horizon. A few hours later, go outside and measure the Moon's width compared to the same finger when the Moon is a lot higher in the sky. Is this size difference real or is it an optical illusion?

Determining Directions

Time

20 minutes

Materials

- 1 thin stick about 12 inches (30 cm) long
- 2 more straight sticks about 12 to 18 inches (30 to 45 cm) long
- 1 ball of clay about 3 inches (8 cm) in diameter
- 2 small rocks or other small objects
- 4 pieces of paper; mark the first with N, the second with S, the third with E, and the fourth with W

Safety Tips and Setup Hints

- You'll need a fairly sunny day for this lab, but a day with some clouds may work, too.
- **Never look directly at the Sun!** Doing so may *very quickly* cause eye damage or blindness.
- Choose an observation spot that is fairly flat and clear of large objects, such as trees or fences, which might cast shadows on it.

Use the Sun and some simple materials to find the cardinal directions: north, south, east, and west.

Instructions

Step 1: Start this lab around midday. The exact time does not matter.

Step 2: Push the end of the 12-inch (30 cm) stick into the ground. If your observation spot is on a hard surface, press the end of your stick into the ball of clay to hold it upright. If the stick doesn't stand up by itself, add a little more clay.

Step 3: Look for the shadow of the stick on the ground. Mark the end of the shadow with a small object, such as a rock. (Fig. 1)

Fig. 1: Mark your first shadow spot.

Fig. 2: Mark your second shadow point.

Fig. 3: Determine your east-west line.

Step 4: In about fifteen minutes, mark the shadow again with another small rock. (Fig. 2)

Step 5: Line up your second stick with the two rocks. This is your east-west line. West is in the direction of your first measurement point. East is in the direction of your second measurement point. Put the E and W signs at the correct ends of the stick. (Fig. 3)

Step 6: Place the third stick perpendicular to your east-west stick. This is your north-south line. Face your east-west stick so east is on your right. North will be ahead of you, and south will be to your back. Put your N and S labels on the ground next to the north-south stick. You have found your directions! (Fig. 4)

Step 7: Look around and find landmarks to help you locate the cardinal directions again from this spot in the future. Make notes in your notebook to record your findings. ◆

The Science Behind the Fun

The Earth spins, or rotates, but to a viewer standing on the rotating Earth, the Earth seems to stand still and the Sun appears to rise, travel across the sky, and set. As the Sun appears to move, shadows cast by the Sun also move. We can use these shadow movements to tell us where our directions are.

Of course, you can find your directions with a compass or a GPS-enabled device, such as a smartphone. But what if you don't have either of these tools or your batteries run out? The two-point stick method will work without any technology at all!

Creative Enrichment

Do the streets in your neighborhood line up with the cardinal directions?

Has anyone ever told you the appearance of moss on a tree can help you find your directions? Use your direction information and make some observations of several trees in your area. Record your findings in your notebook. Is this really true?

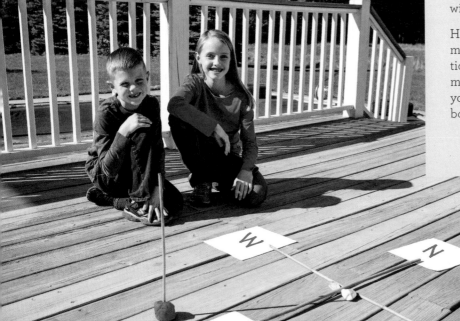

Fig. 4: Success! You found all four directions!

Sunrise, Sunset

Time

5 to 15 minutes per observation, with observations spread throughout the year

Materials

- Your science notebook
- Pencil

Safety Tips and Setup Hints

- **Never look directly at the Sun!** Doing so may *very quickly* cause eye damage or blindness.
- The time of sunrise or sunset may be found in a variety of places, such as in your local newspaper's weather section, the weather portion of your local TV newscast, or online at the U.S. Naval Observatory's website: aa.usno.navy.mil/data/docs/RS_OneDay.php.

Does the Sun always rise in the east and set in the west? Let's find out!

Instructions

Step 1: After learning how to determine east and west in Lab 3, "Determining Directions" (see page 18), choose a spot where you can see to the east or west all the way to the horizon (ideally, a place where you can see both directions). In your notebook, sketch what you see on the horizon to the east and west. Include details, such as buildings, houses, trees, bushes, or any other landmarks. Make sure you can use this same observation site and see the same landmarks each time you do this lab. (Fig. 1)

Step 2: Go to your observation spot about five minutes before sunrise or about five minutes before sunset. Watch for sunrise or sunset and note the location on the horizon where sunrise or sunset occurred. Write the date and time in your notebook to correspond with your observation. Ideally, record the position of sunrise and sunset on the same day, though this may depend on the weather. If you miss a sunrise or sunset observation on the same day, you can go out a day or two later. (Fig. 2)

Step 3: Do these observations for a year and record your data. You can go out once every few days, every few weeks, once per month, or once every couple of months.

The most important dates to observe are on or near December 21, March 21, June 21, and September 22.

Step 4: When you have completed your observations, analyze the data in your notebook. Does the Sun appear to rise directly in the east every day? Does it appear to set directly in the west every day?

Fig. 1: Record data about your observation spot.

Fig. 2: Where does the Sun appear to rise? Where does it appear to set?

The Science Behind the Fun

The positions of sunrise and sunset change throughout the year because the Earth's axis is tilted. The Earth's axis is the imaginary line running from the North Pole to the South Pole directly through the center of the Earth. If the Earth stood straight up and down on its axis, the Sun would appear to rise directly east and set directly west every day. However, because the Earth's axis is tilted at 23.5 degrees and the Earth revolves around the Sun, the positions of sunrise and sunset change throughout the year. The Sun appears to rise directly east and set directly west only on two dates during the year, the spring and fall equinoxes in March and September. How far the positions of sunrise and sunset stray directly from east and west depends on the latitude—the distance north or south of the equator—of the observer.

Creative Enrichment

Do you know someone who lives in another city or country? On or near the same dates, do some sunrise and sunset observations and compare your data. Record the latitude of both of your locations. What similarities and differences do you notice?

To find your latitude, use NASA's Latitude/Longitude Finder: mynasadata.larc.nasa.gov/latitudelongitude-finder

The Sun Above Your Head

Time

5 to 10 minutes per observation, once per month for a year

Materials

- Ruler or measuring tape
- Your science notebook
- Pencil

Safety Tips and Setup Hints

- You'll need a fairly sunny day for this lab, but a day with some clouds may work, too.
- **Never look directly at the Sun!** Doing so may *very quickly* cause eye damage or blindness.
- You'll need a flat surface for this lab, such as a sidewalk or a driveway.
- The lab requires two people, the "Shadow Maker" and the "Measurement Maker." The Shadow Maker should stand in the same spot facing the same direction each time a measurement is made.
- If you are interested in knowing your latitude, use NASA's Latitude/Longitude Finder: mynasadata.larc.nasa.gov/latitudelongitude-finder

At "local noon," does the Sun appear directly overhead where you live?

Fig. 1: Find the time of local noon.

Fig. 2: Measure the length of the Shadow Maker's shadow.

Instructions

Step 1: You will need to do this lab when the Sun is highest in the sky, also called "local noon." To find the time of local noon in your area, go to the U.S. Naval Observatory's website, aa.usno.navy.mil/data/docs/RS_OneDay.php, and enter the date you will do your observation and your location in the form fields. Click the "Get Data" button. On the page that comes up, look for the time of "Sun transit." This is the time the Sun appears highest in the sky where you are located, also called "local noon." (Fig. 1)

Step 2: A few minutes before the time of Sun transit, go to your observation spot. At the time of Sun transit, the Shadow Maker should stand tall and face south. The Measurement Maker will measure the length of the shadow from the Shadow Maker's feet to the end of the longest point on the shadow, which will be the shadow cast by the Shadow Maker's head. Record this shadow length in your science notebook, along with the date and time. (Fig. 2)

Step 3: Repeat these steps about once per month, using the same person as the Shadow Maker each time. The key date to make your observation is the first day of summer, called the "summer solstice." In the Northern Hemisphere, this is around June 21 each year. In the Southern Hemisphere, it is around December 21 each year. Try to make your shadow length observation on the solstice, though doing so a few days before or after will be fine. (Fig. 3)

Step 4: Analyze your data. If the Sun is directly overhead at your spot at some point during the year, you will see the Shadow Maker has cast no extended shadow. In other words, the shadow length will be zero, and the shadow would be right at the Shadow Maker's feet. Is the Sun directly overhead at your location?

Fig. 3: Head out to measure your shadow around the first day of summer.

The Science Behind the Fun

Because the Earth's axis is tilted at 23.5 degrees, for latitudes between 23.5 degrees north and 23.5 degrees south, the Sun appears directly overhead at some point during the year. For the latitude of 23.5 degrees north, the Sun appears directly overhead at the Northern Hemisphere summer solstice on or near June 20 or June 21. For the latitude of 23.5 degrees south, the Sun appears directly overhead at the Southern Hemisphere summer solstice, which is on or near December 21 or 22. There are special names for these special latitudes: 23.5 degrees north latitude is known as the Tropic of Cancer, and 23.5 degrees south latitude is known as the Tropic of Capricorn. For all latitudes north of 23.5 degrees north and all latitudes south of 23.5 degrees south, the Sun never appears directly overhead. It might look close to being overhead, but it isn't!

Creative Enrichment

Do you know someone who lives in another city or country? On or near the same dates, do your shadow length observations and compare your data. Record the latitude of both of your locations. What do you notice?

Our Colorful Sun

Time

20 minutes

Materials

- 1 small ball of white play dough, play clay, or air-dry clay
- 1 (10-inch, or 25 cm) clear hot melt glue stick cut into 2 pieces (see Setup Hint)
- Duct tape
- 1 piece of cardboard 8 inches (20 cm) on a side
- Small white LED flashlight, ideally with a light about the same size as the glue stick

Safety Tips and Setup Hints

- An adult will need to use a sharp blade to cut the hot melt glue stick. One piece should be about 1 inch (2.5 cm) long, and the other piece should be about 4 inches (10 cm) long.
- Shape the small ball of play dough into a cube the same width as the glue stick. Let the cube sit out for a while until it is dry.

Our Sun is yellow, right? Are you sure? Seeing can be deceiving.

Fig. 1: Fasten your clay cube to the cardboard.

Fig. 2: Attach the glue stick pieces to the cardboard.

Instructions

Step 1: Attach the clay cube in the center of the piece of cardboard with duct tape. (Fig. 1)

Step 2: Attach the shorter glue stick piece so it sits about ½ inch (1 cm) above the top of your cube. Attach the longer glue stick piece about ½ inch (1 cm) to the right of the cube. (Fig. 2)

Step 3: Turn on the flashlight and turn off the lights in the room. Notice the color of the light coming from the flashlight. Now, hold the flashlight up against the small glue stick piece so light shines on the cube. What color is the light shining on the cube? (Fig. 3)

Step 4: Hold the flashlight up against the longer glue stick piece so the light shines on the cube. What color is the light shining on the cube? (Fig. 4) ✦

Fig. 3: See the color of the light shining through the small glue stick?

Fig. 4: Is the color of the light shining through the longer glue stick the same?

Creative Enrichment

Japan is called the "land of the rising Sun." What color does the rising Sun appear to be? What is the object depicted on the national flag of Japan? Create a collage of other flags of the world that depict the Sun and research the stories behind the use of the Sun in those flags.

The Science Behind the Fun

Have you seen a rainbow? What colors did you see? These are the colors that make up the light from our Sun. The light our eyes can detect is called "visible light." When all the light from all these colors is viewed together, the light from the Sun appears white. We also call this visible light "white light."

When the Sun's light hits air high up in our atmosphere, the air scatters the blue light. This blue light is what we see from the ground as a blue-colored sky (we'll show this again in Lab 24, "Why is the Sky Blue?" [see page 74]). Because the blue light from the Sun is scattered, our Sun looks more yellow because this blue light has been, basically, "removed." When the Sun is really low in the sky, sunlight passes through even more air and scatters even more of the blue light from the Sun, leaving mostly orange and red light. This leaves our Sun looking redder.

In this lab, the shorter glue stick represents the air above us and the longer glue stick represents the air toward the horizon. The shorter piece scatters blue light from the flashlight, making the light on the cube look a little more yellow. The longer piece scatters even more blue light, making the light on the cube look a little redder. So, what color is our Sun? Is it yellow? Orange? Red? The flashlight gives us the best clue. Depending on how much glue stick the white light passed through, the light at the end appeared different, but the white light from the flashlight itself didn't change. Our Sun really is white! If you were an astronaut in space, the Sun would look white.

Our Changing Moon

 ### Time
10 minutes

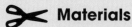 ### Materials

- Chair
- 1 bright lamp with the shade removed or a flashlight
- 1 round, white polystyrene ball at least 2 inches (5 cm) in diameter (your "Moon")
- Your science notebook
- Pencil

 ### Safety Tips and Setup Hints

- This lab requires two people, one person to hold the ball, the "Modeler," and one person to make observations of the phases, the "Observer."
- Do not use Styrofoam balls for this lab; the rough texture of Styrofoam will make the line between the shadow and bright areas harder to see. Polystyrene balls should be available at craft stores.

(Continues on page 28)

Why does our Moon appear to be different shapes? Spin around and see!

Instructions

Step 1: Observer, place the chair in the middle of the room and sit in it. You represent someone standing on the Earth observing the Moon as it goes around you.

Modeler, hold the Moon ball away from you at the same height as the top of the Observer's head and do not let it fall lower than the Observer's eye level. Walk in a circle about 5 feet (1.5 m) from the Observer. (Fig. 1)

Step 2: Modeler, hold the Moon ball in between the Observer and the light.

Observer, look for the Moon ball. Do you see any of the lit part? No! This is the Moon phase called "New Moon." The Moon is in the same part of the sky as the Sun.

Step 3: Modeler, walk a short distance around the Observer in a counterclockwise circle.

Observer, tell the Modeler to stop when you see a small bit of the right side of the Moon ball lit by the lamp. This Moon phase is called "Crescent Moon." (Fig. 2)

Step 4: Modeler, walk a little farther.

Observer, tell the Modeler to stop when you see the right half of the Moon ball lit by the lamp. This Moon phase is called "First Quarter Moon." (Fig. 3)

(Continues on page 28)

Fig. 1: The Modeler walks the Moon ball around the Observer.

Fig. 2: See the little bit of light on the right side?

Fig. 3: This is First Quarter Moon.

Safety Tips and Setup Hints

(Continued from page 26)

- If the polystyrene ball does not have a small hole in the bottom, an adult should drill a hole just large enough so the pencil can fit. The pencil will be your handle.

- For this lab, use a room that can be completely darkened. Place the bright light at one end of the room.

Step 5: Modeler, walk a little more.

Observer, tell the Modeler to stop when you see most of the right side of the Moon ball lit by the lamp. This Moon phase is called "Gibbous Moon" (pronounced GIB-bus).

Step 6: Modeler, walk a little farther around the Observer.

Observer, tell the Modeler to stop when you see the entire side of the Moon ball facing you lit by the lamp. This Moon phase is called "Full Moon." (Fig. 4)

Step 7: Modeler, walk a little farther around the Observer.

Observer, tell the Modeler to stop when you see most of the left side of the Moon ball lit by the lamp. This is also a "Gibbous Moon."

Step 8: Modeler, keep going a little farther.

Observer, tell the Modeler to stop when you see the left half of the Moon ball lit by the lamp. This phase is called "Third Quarter Moon." (Fig. 5)

Step 9: Modeler, keep going in a circle.

Observer, tell the Modeler to stop when you see a sliver of the Moon ball on the left side lit by the lamp. This phase is also called a "Crescent Moon." (Fig. 6)

Step 10: Modeler, you should return to holding the Moon ball in the same part of the Observer's view as the lamp. This, again, is the New Moon. ✦

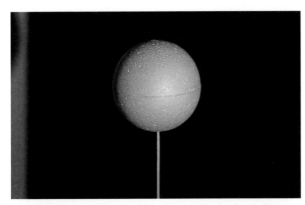

Fig. 4: Full Moon is when the Moon is opposite the Sun in the sky—as the Sun sets, the Full Moon rises.

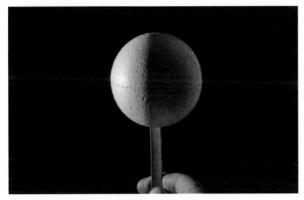

Fig. 5: See the lit left half of the Moon ball?

Fig. 6: See the little bit of light on the left side?

The Science Behind the Fun

Just as the Earth moves around the Sun, our Moon orbits the Earth. Two other terms for "moves around" are "revolves around" or "orbits." The time it takes for the Moon to orbit the Earth once is approximately 29½ Earth days. In other words, the Earth spins 29½ times in the time it takes for the Moon to go around the Earth once. Half of the Moon is always lit by the Sun, and Moon phases are just the changing amount of the Moon that is lit by the Sun *as seen from Earth*.

Creative Enrichment

The name "dark side of the Moon" has been used by some people to describe the side of the Moon that faces away from the Earth. Is this an appropriate name? Why or why not?

LAB 08

Eclipse the Sun, Eclipse the Moon

Time

5 minutes

Materials

- This lab uses the same materials as Lab 7, "Our Changing Moon" (see page 26), plus more in this list.
- Small white LED flashlight, such as a penlight flashlight. The flashlight used for Lab 6, "Our Colorful Sun" (see page 24), would work well, too.
- Very small ball of play dough or play clay, no larger than ½ inch (1 cm) in diameter

Safety Tips and Setup Hints

- Please follow the same "Safety Tips and Setup Hints" as Lab 7, "Our Changing Moon" (see page 26).
- Remember always to move the Moon ball in a *counterclockwise* direction around the Observer. This represents the direction the Moon orbits the Earth.

What is an eclipse? When can I see one?

Fig. 1: When the Sun is blocked by the Moon, this is a solar eclipse.

Instructions

Step 1: Modeler, hold the Moon ball so it is in the same part of the Observer's view as the lamp bulb, as you did for the phase known as New Moon. This time, try to block the light from the Sun lamp so the Observer cannot see the lamp bulb.

Observer, tell the Modeler when the light from the lamp is fully blocked by the Moon ball. When the Moon fully covers the Sun as seen from Earth, this is called a "total solar eclipse." Observer, work with the Modeler to find a spot when the Moon ball partly covers the lightbulb so you can see just a bit of the light coming from the lamp. When the Moon covers only part of the Sun as seen from Earth, this is called a "partial solar eclipse." (Fig. 1)

Fig. 2: During a lunar eclipse, the Moon appears darker.

Fig. 3: Transits only cover a tiny part of the Sun.

Step 2: Modeler, hold the Moon ball as you did for the Full Moon phase, with the Moon ball on one side of the Observer and the lamp on the opposite side.

Observer, tell the Modeler when the Moon ball passes through the shadow cast by your head. When the Moon passes through the shadow cast by the Earth, this is called a "lunar eclipse." If the Moon partly passes through the Earth's shadow but the other part of it is still lit by the Sun, this is called a "partial lunar eclipse." If the Moon fully passes through the Earth's shadow, this is called a "total lunar eclipse." (Fig. 2)

Step 3: Modeler, put the Moon ball down and pick up the small ball of play clay. Stand about 5 feet (1.5 m) from the Observer. Move the ball so it passes between the Observer and the light, blocking a little bit of the light as seen by the Observer, but not all the light. When an object passes in front of the Sun but it is too small to cover the Sun completely, this is called a "transit." (Fig. 3)

Creative Enrichment

The next time the planet Mercury will transit the Sun will be in 2019. See if this event will be visible in your area: aa.usno.navy.mil/data/docs/UpcomingTransits.php.

A few weeks before the transit, inquire if a local planetarium or astronomy club is planning to provide telescopes to see it. If so, check it out!

The Science Behind the Fun

An eclipse of the Sun occurs when the Moon passes between the Sun and an Observer on Earth. In our model, the Moon ball passed in front of the light, blocking it completely, and the shadow of the Moon ball fell on the Observer. These solar eclipses can occur only at the New Moon phase, when the Moon is in the same part of the sky as the Sun.

An eclipse of the Moon occurs when the Moon passes through the shadow cast by the Earth. In our model, the Moon ball passed through the shadow cast by the Observer's head. Lunar eclipses can only occur at the Full Moon phase, when the Moon is on the opposite side of the Earth as the Sun.

A "transit" occurs when an object passes between a star and an Observer, but the object does not completely cover and block all the light from the star. One of the more well-known transits is the Transit of Venus, when Venus passes between the Sun and the Earth. Venus can be seen as a small dot against the larger Sun. The last two Transits of Venus occurred in 2004 and 2012. The next one will be in 2117. Transits are also used by astronomers to find planets around other stars, as the distant planet blocks a tiny bit of light from its star. We see this effect as a temporary dimming of light from the star.

Twinkle, Twinkle

Time

10 minutes

Materials

- 1 clear glass bowl or container that holds at least 6 cups (1.5 liters) of liquid
- 4 cups (1 L) of cold water
- Small flashlight; the flashlight used for Lab 6, "Our Colorful Sun" (see page 24) would work well.
- 2 cups (500 ml) of warm water

Safety Tips and Setup Hints

- Use a darkened room for this lab.
- The twinkling effect will be more pronounced if the difference in temperature between the cold water and warm water is wider. Use hot tap water for the warm water, and put ice cubes into the cold water for a while. Be careful! The temperature of hot tap water is sometimes enough to cause burns.

Stars seem to twinkle, but why?

Instructions

Step 1: Pour the cold water into the bowl (without the ice cubes), and let the water settle so it is not moving. Don't fill up the bowl because you will need to pour more water in later. Turn on the flashlight and turn off the lights in the room. (Fig. 1)

Step 2: Point the flashlight at the bowl and bend down so you can see the light from the flashlight as you look through the side of the bowl and through the water. Place the flashlight about 12 inches (30 cm) from the bowl. Observe the light from the flashlight through the water. (Fig. 2)

Step 3: Slowly and carefully pour the warm water into the bowl, and again observe the light through the water. (It might help to have someone else pour the water for you.) What does pouring the warm water into the bowl do to the beam of light from the flashlight? (Fig. 3)

Step 4: This time, place the flashlight across the room at least 10 feet (3 m) from the bowl. Pour out all the water from the bowl. Replenish your amounts of cold and hot water and repeat the experiment. What do you notice about the beam of light when the flashlight is farther from the bowl? If you have room, keep repeating the experiment, moving the flashlight farther from the bowl each time. (Fig. 4) ◆

Fig. 3: Pour the warm water in. What do you see?

Fig. 4: The light is farther away. Now what do you see?

Fig. 1: Let the cold water settle in the bowl.

Fig. 2: Observe the light as it goes through the water.

Creative Enrichment

When we look at planets in our Solar System from Earth, they do not seem to twinkle much at all. Why not? *Hint: How far away are planets in our Solar System compared to the stars we see at night?* Use an online star map or phone application to find when and where a planet, such as Venus, might be visible and compare its beam of light to that of a twinkling star.

Note: While this enrichment idea works for other planets such as Mercury, Mars, Jupiter, and Saturn, Venus will be the easiest object to spot because it will be brighter than anything else in the early morning or early evening sky—other than the Moon. If you don't know how to find planets in the sky, it is best to start practicing with Venus!

The Science Behind the Fun

When you go outside on a clear night, look up. Do you see stars? If so, watch them for a little while. What do you see? Chances are, if you watch long enough, the light from the stars will seem to wiggle or move a tiny bit. This is twinkling!

Stars are very large, but they are very, very far away, so they appear as tiny points in the sky. The tiny beam of light from a star passes through Earth's air to where you are standing on the ground. The air above you moves around a lot. It is this moving air that causes the beam of light to move around a bit.

Sometimes when you look at a twinkling star, it will appear to change color. Is the star actually changing color right before your eyes? No. A star's light contains all colors, from red, orange, and yellow to green, blue, and violet. Sometimes the colors of light from a star will twinkle differently, making the star appear to be one color, then another, and still another. This is especially easy to see with very bright stars viewed when they are closer to the horizon, as you are seeing them through more of Earth's air.

If you look at a star from space, will it twinkle? No! Because there is no air in space, there is nothing to cause the star's light to jiggle. The light from stars would appear steady if you saw them from space. This is why the Hubble Space Telescope has been such an amazing machine. It orbits above the blurring effects of Earth's air.

Scope It Out!

Many people think Galileo was the inventor of the telescope, but he was not. In 1608 Dutch lens makers were likely the first to do so. Galileo heard about this wonderful tool, and he worked to improve it. In 1609 he pointed his telescope at objects in the sky and kept a notebook of his observations.

Over many weeks and months, Galileo saw jagged mountains and craters on the Moon and phases of Venus that looked like phases of our Moon. He observed four objects that orbited the planet Jupiter, what we know to be Jupiter's four largest moons. He saw stars not visible to the naked eye, and more. In 1610 he published his observations in a book called *Starry Messenger*.

Telescopes seem complicated, don't they? Almost like magic, special lenses and mirrors show us things in the sky we didn't see before. It isn't magic, though. It's science! Let's use some simple materials to make these tools easier to understand.

On May 13, 2009, NASA astronauts on the space shuttle *Atlantis* captured this view of the Hubble Space Telescope against the backdrop of Earth.
Credit: NASA

Bend Light with Ice

Time

2 to 4 hours

Materials

- 1 very sharp knife, such as a box cutter
- 1 racquetball or tennis ball
- 1 plastic container just slightly larger than the ball
- Distilled water
- 1 flat page with printed words, such as a piece of newspaper or a page cut from a magazine
- Plastic wrap
- 1 large metal spoon

Safety Tips and Setup Hints

- An adult should cut the ball in half with the sharp knife.
- Distilled water is available from the grocery store or from pharmacies.
- The amount of time needed for this lab will depend on the time it takes for the water to freeze in your freezer.
- If your ice is cloudy, you will have to start over. Don't be discouraged if you need more than one try to make a clear (or mostly clear) ice lens. That's the fun part about science—try and try again!

Magnifying glass? How about "magnifying ice?"

Instructions

Step 1: Place one ball half into a container with the rounded edge facing down. Fill the hollow part of the ball with distilled water just to the top. (Fig. 1)

Step 2: Without spilling the water, place the container with the filled ball half into the freezer. Check it every hour or so until the water is frozen. Do not leave it in the freezer very long after the water freezes or the ice will get cloudy.

Step 3: When the ice is frozen solid, carefully remove the ice lens from the ball half. You might need to run warm water over the outside of the ball to loosen the lens. Rub the flat side of your ice lens with your hand. The heat from your hand will smooth out that flat side. (Fig. 2)

Step 4: Lay the newspaper or magazine page on the table with the printed words facing up. Place the plastic wrap on top of the page. Smooth out any wrinkles in the paper or plastic.

Step 5: Place the ice lens on the plastic so you can see words through it. Lift the lens from the paper to see the effect. What do you notice? (Fig. 3)

Step 6: Grab a large metal spoon. Look at your own reflection from both sides of the metal spoon. How does your reflection on the front of the spoon look different from your reflection on the back of the spoon? Compare the view of the words through the lens to the reflection you see from both sides of the metal spoon. Which reflection and lens view look similar?

Fig. 1: Fill the inside of the ball with water.

The Science Behind the Fun

In this lab, you used objects with different types of curvature. We call those curvature types "concave" and "convex." A lens or mirror with a middle that bulges outward is called "convex." A lens or a mirror with a middle that curves inward is called "concave." An easy way to try to remember these words is that concave is like a cave that is carved inward into a mountain. The other shape is convex. The lens you made is a convex lens.

A convex lens and a concave mirror have the same effect on rays of light: both cause images to look bigger. A magnifying glass is a great example of a convex lens. A concave lens and a convex mirror also have the same effect on rays of light: both cause images to look smaller. The bending of light though a clear lens is called "refracting." When light bounces off a mirror, this bouncing of light is called "reflecting."

Fig. 2: A lens made of ice!

Fig. 3: Look through your lens. What do you see?

Creative Enrichment

Can you figure out a way to make a concave ice lens? Try carefully floating the ball half on top of the water as you freeze the water into a cave shape, or try CAREFULLY melting a cave shape into a small block of ice, or see if you can come up with another way that might work. This may be very hard, but see if you can do it! There is no one right answer. (Remember, if any of your ideas involve knives or sharp objects, make sure an adult is there to help you!)

LAB 11

Focus!

Time

15 minutes

Materials

- 1 lamp with the shade removed, showing just the bare bulb
- 1 lens from a pair of drugstore reading glasses (+1.00, +1.25, or +1.50 strength)
- Painter's tape or masking tape
- 1 sheet of white copy paper
- Tape measure
- Magnifying glass

Safety Tips and Setup Hints

- You will need to arrange the bulb in the lamp, plus one of the lenses from the eyeglasses, and the sheet of paper in a straight line. When you set up the lens and the bulb, try to get them at exactly the same height, and hold the paper at the same height.

- Two people are needed for this lab, one to move and hold the paper and one to measure the distance from the lens to the paper.

- It helps to do this lab in a darkened room.

Focus your attention on these lenses!

Fig. 1: Set up the bulb and the lens.

Fig. 2: The bulb, then the lens, then the piece of paper are all in a straight line.

Fig. 3: Look for a very tiny view of the lightbulb on the paper.

Instructions

Step 1: Turn on the lamp and put it at one end of the room. Turn off the other room lights.

Step 2: Tape the reading glasses to the side of something sturdy, like the back of a chair, so one of the lenses sticks up or out to the side. Place this lens at least 10 feet (3 m) from the lightbulb. Farther away is even better. Keep the lens and the bulb at the same height. (Fig. 1)

Step 3: Hold the piece of paper in line with the lens so it is on the opposite side of the lens as the bulb. (Fig. 2)

Fig. 4: Measure the lens-to-paper distance.

Step 4: Move the paper away from the lens, keeping it in a straight line with the bulb and the lens, until you see a very small image of the lit lightbulb on the paper. (Fig. 3)

Step 5: Continue to hold the paper in this spot. Use the tape measure to measure the distance between the lens and the paper. What is the distance that you measured? (Fig. 4)

Step 6: Replace this lens with the lens from the magnifying glass. Repeat steps 2, 3, and 4 with this lens. What is this distance? How does it compare with the distance you measured using the first lens?

Step 7: Feel the glasses lens and then feel the magnifying glass lens. Which one is thicker in the middle? Which lens had the shorter distance that you measured? ◆

The Science Behind the Fun

As was shown in Lab 10, "Bend Light with Ice" (see page 36), lenses thicker in the middle that curve outward are called "convex" lenses. Convex lenses bring light together at a specific spot. The image of the object at this spot is tiny and in focus. The spot at which convex lenses bring light to a focus is called the "focal point." The distance between the lens and this focal point is called the "focal length." You can measure the focal length of convex lenses by measuring the distance between the lens and the focused spot. Concave mirrors also have a focal point.

Creative Enrichment

Can you determine the focal length of the convex ice lens you created in Lab 10, "Bend Light with Ice" (see page 36)? If you created more than one convex ice lens, can you measure the focal lengths of those lenses? Work quickly, or your ice lenses will melt and change shape! This may be hard!

Did you notice the small image of the lightbulb was upside down? Is this a mistake? Try observing the light from different sources, such as another bulb, a flashlight, or a television. What did you find?

LAB 12

Fuzzy Color

Time

10 minutes

Materials

- 1 round, clear glass fishbowl filled with water
- 1 bright lamp with the shade removed, showing just the bare bulb
- 1 sheet of white copy paper

Safety Tips and Setup Hints

- Do not use the Sun as the light source for this lab. If the fishbowl is in the right location, it may focus the light rays from the Sun, causing the paper to burn. Use a lamp in a room that can be darkened; the darker the room, the easier it will be to see the image formed on the paper.

- You will need to arrange the lamp bulb, the fishbowl, and the sheet of paper in a straight line. When you set them up, try to get them all at the same height.

- While a glass bowl might work somewhat well for this lab, try to find an actual round-shaped fishbowl. It will work the best.

- It helps to do this lab in a darkened room.

Lenses can have fuzzy problems, as this lab colorfully shows.

Instructions

Step 1: Place the fishbowl filled with water onto a table or counter. Turn on the lamp and put it at one end of the room at least 10 feet (3 m) from the fishbowl. Turn off the other room lights. (Fig. 1)

Step 2: Hold the copy paper upright on the opposite side of the fishbowl as the lamp. (Fig. 2)

Step 3: Pull the paper away from the fishbowl until you see an image of the bulb. Which part of the bulb is at the top of the image? If you can, carefully move the bulb upward slightly, then downward. What does this do to the image of the bulb on the paper? (Note: Depending on the shape of the fishbowl and the thickness of the glass, this may be difficult to see. Keep trying, though!) (Fig. 3)

Step 4: Next, observe the color of the image of the bulb and the colors around the image. What do you see?

Step 5: The last thing to observe is the sharpness of the image of the bulb. What do you see in the middle of the image? What about at the edges of the image? ✦

Fig. 1: Get your fishbowl ready.

Fig. 2: Hold your screen (copy paper) in line with the fishbowl and lamp.

Creative Enrichment

Look around the house to see if you can find any other materials that might make good convex lenses. Can they focus the light from a bulb or from a television? Give them a try!

Fig. 3: See the image of the bulb?

The Science Behind the Fun

In this lab, the fishbowl filled with water was a convex lens! As you saw in Lab 10, "Bend Light with Ice" (see page 36), lenses come in two main shapes, concave and convex. The centers of concave lenses bulge inward and the centers of convex lenses bulge outward. A perfect convex lens is supposed to bring light together so all the light is bent toward a small spot; as you learned in Lab 11, "Focus!" (see page 38), this small spot is the "focal point" and the distance from the lens to this point is the "focal length." In reality, though, lenses are not perfect. They do not bring light to a single point because different rays of light are bent by lenses in different ways. The problems that we see with convex lenses can show a fuzzy image or an image with colors that look strange.

When you saw the image of the bulb or the light that shone through the glass, did you see colors on the edges of your image on the paper? This color problem occurs because different colors of light, such as blue, green, or red, are each bent slightly differently by a lens. There is one focal point for blue light, a slightly farther focal point for green light, and an even farther focal point for red light. In the image created by our fishbowl lens, this is not much of an issue, but it is a problem when astronomers use telescopes with lenses to look at faraway objects, such as stars. Astronomers want images of objects without rings of color around them. To correct this problem, some telescope lenses contain a few different kinds of glass. Each type of glass brings a different color of light to the same focal point, and all these glass types work together to create an image with as few colorful edges as possible.

Make a Simple Telescope

Time
10 minutes

Materials
- 1 lamp with the shade removed, showing just the bare bulb
- 1 lens from a pair of drugstore reading glasses (+1.00, +1.25, or +1.50 strength)
- Painter's tape or masking tape
- 1 sheet of white copy paper
- Magnifying glass

Safety Tips and Setup Hints
- Do not use the Sun as the light source for this lab. The lens will focus the light rays from the Sun, causing the paper to burn. It would also damage your eyes very quickly.
- Note that the lightbulb used in the pictures for this lab is brighter than what you will need to use. Use a dim bulb or flashlight so it isn't too bright when you look at it through the lenses.
- The first three steps of this lab are the same as for Lab 11, "Focus!" (see page 38).

Telescopes seem complicated, but making this one is about as easy as you can get!

Instructions

Step 1: Turn on the lamp and put it at one end of the room. Turn off the other room lights.

Step 2: Tape the reading glasses to the side of something sturdy, like the back of a chair, so one of the lenses sticks outward or upward. Place this lens at least 10 feet (3 m) from the lightbulb (farther away is even better). Keep the lens and the bulb at the same height. (Fig. 1)

Step 3: Hold the piece of paper in line with the lens on the opposite side of the lens as the lamp—the lamp, then the lens, then the piece of paper. Move the paper away from the lens, keeping it in a straight line with the bulb and lamp, until you see a very small image of the lit lightbulb on the paper. (Fig. 2)

Step 4: When you see a focused tiny image, hold the magnifying glass exactly where the paper shows the image of the bulb, and then take the paper away. Keep holding the magnifying glass in this spot. Put your eye up to the magnifying glass, as if you were looking through a telescope. Look through the magnifying glass at the image of the bulb, and pull your eye away very slowly until you see a slightly larger—and brighter—image of the bulb. (Fig. 3) ✦

Fig. 1: Set up the bulb and the lens.

Fig. 2: Look for a very tiny image of the lightbulb on the paper.

Creative Enrichment

Try constructing a tube system to hold your lenses apart at the correct distance. You may need to have the ability for the eyepiece lens to slide toward and away from the objective lens so you can focus your image. Can you take your telescope outside and use it? (Just don't point it at the Sun!)

The Science Behind the Fun

A telescope with a lens at the front and another lens at the back is called a "refractor." The lens at the front of a refractor telescope is known as the "objective" lens. This lens gathers light from the object and bends, or refracts, it, bringing the light together to form a very tiny image of the object. The larger the objective lens, the more light that can be gathered and the brighter the object will appear. The lens at the back is known as the "eyepiece." The eyepiece lens magnifies the tiny image from the objective lens so your eye can see it easily. You can change the magnification of a telescope by changing the eyepiece.

What do you think of when you see the word *telescope*? Do you think of a tube with a lens at the front and back? Many people do. There is another type of telescope—a "reflector" telescope, which uses a curved mirror (or several mirrors) as the objective lens to gather light. There are also one or more smaller mirrors to reflect the light toward the eyepiece lens.

These days, most refractor telescopes use convex lenses for the objective and the eyepiece. Scientist Johannes Kepler perfected this type of telescope, so this type is called "Keplerian." Galileo's telescope used a convex objective lens and a concave eyepiece lens, so this type is called "Galilean." Reflector telescopes use a concave objective mirror and a convex eyepiece, and there are several different arrangements of smaller flat or curved mirrors to get the light to the eyepiece.

Fig. 3: Do you see the image?

Make a Pinhole Projector

Time
15 minutes

Materials
- 1 long cardboard box (or more than one box taped together); the width and height are not particularly important, but the length should be at least 5 feet (1.5 m)
- Box cutter or a pair of very sharp, sturdy scissors
- 1 piece of aluminum foil about 6 inches (15 cm) on a side
- Pin, tack, or pushpin
- 1 sheet of white copy paper
- Masking tape, duct tape, or packing tape
- Small ruler (optional)

Safety Tips and Setup Hints
- You'll need a fairly sunny day for this lab.
- **Never look directly at the Sun**, and do not look through your pinhole or through your pinhole projector at the Sun! Doing so may *very quickly* cause eye damage or blindness.
- An adult should do any cutting using the scissors or box cutter. They can be extremely sharp.

Do you need a fancy camera to see an image of the Sun? No! Would you believe it's as easy as a pin?

Fig. 5: Point the pinhole at the Sun and look for an image on your screen.

Fig. 6: Here comes the Sun!

Instructions

Step 1: In the middle of one end of the box, measure a hole that is about 2 by 2 inches (5 by 5 cm) square. The hole does not have to be exactly in the middle of the end of the box, nor does the hole have to be exactly square. Cut out this hole and discard the piece you cut out. (Fig. 1)

Step 2: Securely tape the aluminum foil over the hole. Try to make the foil as smooth as possible. (Fig. 2)

Fig. 1: Cut the hole out of one end of the box.

Fig. 2: Tape aluminum foil over the hole.

Fig. 3: Punch a pinhole into the foil.

Step 3: Using the pin, carefully punch a small hole into the middle of the aluminum foil. Keep the hole the size of the pin itself. (Fig. 3)

Step 4: Opposite the pinhole end, cut open a flap in the side of the box and tape a sheet of white paper across the inside end of the box opposite the pinhole end. This is your "screen" where you will project the Sun's image. (Fig. 4)

Step 5: You can try out your pinhole projector inside using a bright lightbulb. Turn on the lightbulb, darken the room, point the pinhole end of the box at the lightbulb, and look for a small image of the bulb on the white sheet of paper. It may take a little practice. Don't get your head in the way!

Step 6: Once you are good at using your projector inside with lightbulbs, go outside and try to project an image of the Sun. You may find you will need to prop your box on a fence post, a deck railing, or some other sturdy object. Once you find the Sun successfully, it should get easier to do so repeatedly. (Figs. 5, 6) ◆

Fig. 4: Tape your "screen" inside the other end of your box.

The Science Behind the Fun

While everyone is probably most familiar with glass or plastic lenses as a way to make a sharp image of something, you can simply use a pinhole. The pinhole acts like a tiny lens, allowing an image of something bright to be seen at some distance from the pinhole.

You need a very long box for this lab. The size of the image of the Sun that the pinhole projects is only going to be about 1 percent of the length of the box. That means that for a box 60 inches (5 feet, or 1.5 m) in length, the image of the Sun the pinhole produces is only going to be 0.6 inches (1.5 cm) in diameter.

Creative Enrichment

When you look at the images of lightbulbs on your "screen," how are the images oriented? Are they right side up?

Try playing with several sizes of pinholes. What happens to the size or brightness of your image? Next, try changing the length of your projector box. If you keep your pinhole size the same but your projector box is longer or shorter, what happens to your image? Is there a "perfect" hole size for a certain length of projector box?

Size and Scale

How big is it? How far is it? These are questions we ask a lot. It can be hard to wrap our minds around big sizes or huge distances, especially for things in space. Something bright and far can look like something that is dim and close. Something small and near could look like something that is big and distant. Without a scale to follow, a small planet in one picture can appear to be the same dimensions as a huge galaxy in another.

To understand things that are big and far better, it is helpful to compare them to things we see every day. Shrink the Earth to the size of a ball, a marble, or maybe the head of a pushpin.

Shrink the Sun to a circle a few feet (a few meters) wide. Shrink the whole Milky Way galaxy to the size of a cookie. Sizes and distances suddenly become a little more reasonable!

The next set of activities compares sizes and distances using various scales and objects. After you are done with this set, go outside and look up! Maybe the Moon, Sun, planets, and stars won't seem quite as far away after all!

If Earth was a 1-inch (2.5 cm) marble, Jupiter would be an 11-inch (28 cm) playground kickball. Nearly 1,000 Earth marbles would fill a kickball Jupiter!

Credit: Image courtesy NASA/JPL-Caltech

How Far Away Is the Moon?

Time

5 minutes

Materials

- 1 container of play dough or play clay
- Small ruler
- Tape measure at least 6 feet (2 m) long

Safety Tips and Setup Hints

- Roll one ball of play dough to about ½ inch (1.5 cm) in diameter. This will be the Moon model.
- Roll one ball of play dough to about 2 inches (5 cm) in diameter. This will be the Earth model.
- This lab requires two people to do, but it is even more fun if more people participate. Gather some family members! For every person who joins in, make another Moon ball model so you have one Moon ball for each person. If you have more than two or three people, you may need one or two more containers of play dough so everyone can have a Moon ball.
- Use a room with open floor space or an outdoor space for this lab.

The Moon is something we all see in the sky. It looks really close to us. But is it?

Instructions

Step 1: Hold the Earth model in one hand, show it to the other lab participants, and identify it as a model of the Earth. Hold a Moon model in your other hand, show it to everyone, and identify it as a model of the Moon. (Fig. 1)

Step 2: Give all participants a Moon ball model to hold. Put the Earth model on a table or chair so everyone can see it.

Step 3: Invite participants to guess how far the Moon is from the Earth, if the Earth and Moon were shrunk to those sizes. Have each person stand with their Moon model as far from the Earth model as they feel the Moon is from the Earth on this scale. (Fig. 2)

Step 4: Once everyone has made their guesses, measure about 60 inches (1.5 m) from the Earth model. Place the remaining Moon model at this distance. How did everyone else's guesses compare to the real scale? ◆

Fig. 1: The ball on the left is the Earth and the ball on the right is the Moon.

Fig. 2: Guess how far the Moon is from the Earth on this scale!

The Science Behind the Fun

Our planet Earth is almost 8,000 miles (12,800 km) in diameter. Our Moon is about 2,200 miles (about 3,475 km) in diameter. In other words, the Earth is just over 3½ times the diameter of the Moon. The Moon does not orbit Earth in a precise circle, but, on average, the Moon orbits Earth at a distance of about 240,000 miles (384,000 km).

So, how do you measure the distance between the Earth and the Moon? Use a very long tape measure? Well, there is one special kind of tape measure we can use: the speed of light. Three of the *Apollo* lunar astronaut crews left special sets of mirrors on the surface of the Moon. These mirrors are called "retroreflectors," and they reflect light straight back to Earth in the direction it came from. Laser light fired from a telescope on Earth travels to the retroreflectors, and the light comes back to a detector at the telescope. Because we know the speed of light, we can measure the amount of time it takes for the light to travel to the Moon and back and, from these two pieces of information, we can figure out the distance.

So, why do we need to know the distance to the Moon? Isn't it usually the same? Surprisingly, no! The laser measurements tell us the Moon is moving away from the Earth at about 1.6 inches (4 cm) per year! This is also a rate similar to the speed that your fingernails grow.

Don't worry, though. The Moon is not about to fly away from the Earth. It will be our companion for a very, very long time!

Creative Enrichment

On average, it takes around 1.3 seconds for a beam of light to travel from the Earth to the Moon and another 1.3 seconds for the light to return. Can you figure out a way to show the speed of light from the Earth to the Moon and back using your Earth-Moon distance model and a timer?

If the Moon is moving away from the Earth at about 1.6 inches (4 cm) per year, how many inches has it moved from the Earth in your lifetime? What about in your relatives' lifetimes? How far will the Moon move away from the Earth in one hundred years? In one thousand years? In one million years?

LAB 16

How Can the Moon Cover the Sun?

Time

10 minutes on a sunny day, 10 minutes on a Full Moon night

Materials

- The pinhole projector you made in Lab 14, "Make a Pinhole Projector" (see page 44)
- Measuring tape at least as long as your pinhole projector
- Pencil
- Ruler
- Your science notebook
- Calculator

Safety Tips and Setup Hints

- You will need a night where you can see the Full Moon. The higher the Moon is above the horizon, the brighter it will appear in your projector.
- **Never look directly at the Sun**, and do not look through your pinhole or through your pinhole projector at the Sun! Doing so may *very quickly* cause eye damage or blindness.
- For this lab, you will need to remove the screen twice from inside your pinhole projector. Lightly tape each paper screen inside your projector.

Our Moon can completely cover the Sun. It is so much smaller than the Sun, so how does that work?

Fig. 1: Point your pinhole projector at the Sun.

Instructions

Step 1: Go outside and project an image of the Sun using your pinhole projector. You may find you need to prop your box on a fence post, a deck railing, or some other sturdy object. (Fig. 1)

Step 2: While one person holds the projector to create an image of the Sun, another person should mark the outer edges of the image on the screen with the pen or pencil. It will help your measurement if you can draw a complete circle around the Sun's image, but if you cannot do this, mark as much of the outer edge as you can. Remove this screen from your projector and write "Sun" on it. Be careful! Try not to tear the paper. Save this screen for later. (Fig. 2)

Step 3: Repeat steps 1 and 2 for the image of the Full Moon. Remove the screen from your projector and write "Moon" on it. Save this screen for later.

Step 4: Measure the distance between the pinhole end of your projector and the screen end of your projector in inches or centimeters. Write down this measurement in your notebook. (Fig. 3)

Step 5: Measure the diameters of your Sun image and your Moon image. Write these measurements in your notebook. Be sure to use the same units as you used to measure the length of your projector (inches or centimeters). (Fig. 4)

Step 6: Grab your calculator, a pen or pencil, and your measurements. First, divide the diameter of your Sun image by the distance from the pinhole to your screen (use the same units!). Write down this number. Multiply this result by the distance between the Earth and the Sun, which is about 93 million miles (or 149,600,000 km). Write down your result.

Step 7: Divide the diameter of your Moon image by the distance from the pinhole to your screen. Write down this number. Multiply this result by the distance between the Earth and the Moon, which is about 239,000 miles (or 384,000 km). Write down your result. Compare this result to your calculation for the Sun. How do they compare? ✦

Fig. 2: Mark the size of the Sun on the screen in the projector.

Fig. 3: Measure the length of your pinhole projector.

Fig. 4: Measure the sizes of your images.

The Science Behind the Fun

The numbers you calculated should be fairly similar. But how does this work? Our Moon is only about 2,150 miles (3,475 km) in diameter, while our Sun is about 865,000 miles (1,390,000 km) in diameter. Our Sun is HUGE compared to the Moon! What's going on?

As you saw in Lab 8, "Eclipse the Sun, Eclipse the Moon" (see page 30), our Moon can completely cover the Sun during a total solar eclipse. If you compare the diameters of the Sun and Moon, the Sun is about 400 times larger than our Moon, but if you compare the distances of the Moon and Sun from Earth, the Sun is about 400 times farther away from us than the Moon. That is how it works!

As you learned in Lab 15, "How Far Away Is the Moon?" (see page 48), our Moon is moving slowly away from Earth at a rate of 1.6 inches (4 cm) a year. At some point, the Moon will be too far from Earth to cover the Sun completely during an eclipse. How many years into the future will this be? Don't worry. It won't be soon. We still have about 600 million years to go!

Creative Enrichment

Find out when the next partial or total lunar or solar eclipse is happening in your area. Plan a family observing trip around it. Be sure to keep a journal of your experiences!

Pennies and Planets

Time

30 minutes

Materials

- Permanent marker
- 11 clean, empty 12-ounce (340 g) aluminum soda cans
- Masking tape or duct tape
- 1,100 pennies ($11 in pennies), or other small coins, such as 1-cent Euros, 1-cent Australian coins, 20-centavo coins from Mexico, and so forth.
- 1 full, same size unopened can of the same liquid

Safety Tips and Setup Hints

- This lab is all about comparison—the weight of an object on Earth compared to the weight of that same object on another world. To get the comparison right, you need to use the same objects, in this case pennies, in all the cans.
- Be careful when you put objects into or remove pennies from the empty cans. The edge of the can's mouth is sharp!

(Continues on page 54)

Here is a use for all those extra pennies or other small coins around your house. You can investigate gravity!

Instructions

Step 1: Using the permanent marker, write "Earth" on the bottom of the full, unopened can. Then, write the name of a planet, moon, or dwarf planet on the bottom of each empty can: Mercury, Venus, Moon, Mars, Ceres, Jupiter, Io, Saturn, Uranus, Neptune, Pluto. (Fig. 1)

Step 2: Fill the labeled cans with the following number of pennies or other small coins (Fig. 2):

Mercury: 53 pennies	Io: 25 pennies
Venus: 127 pennies	Saturn: 151 pennies
Moon: 23 pennies	Uranus: 127 pennies
Mars: 53 pennies	Neptune: 167 pennies
Ceres: 4 pennies	Pluto: 10 pennies
Jupiter: 354 pennies	

(Continues on page 54)

The Science Behind the Fun

People often think Earth is the only place with gravity. This isn't true. Our Moon has gravity, Mars has gravity, Jupiter has gravity . . . every object in space has gravity! Here on Earth, we are used to Earth's pull of gravity. Pick up an object, and you are doing work by pulling against the force of Earth's gravity.

Would your weight change if you went to another world? The weight of an object has to do with the amount of stuff in an object, called its "mass," and the pull of gravity that object feels. If the force of gravity goes up, the object's weight will go up. If the force of gravity is less, the object's weight is less. However, the amount of stuff in the object, its mass, stays the same.

If you traveled to another world, the amount of stuff in you is still exactly the same, but the force of gravity there might be different. So, while your mass will be the same, your weight may change. A full, unopened can of soda on Earth will have exactly the same amount of soda and the same mass on another world, but the can might weigh more or less depending on where you go.

Fig. 1: Label the bottom of each can.

Fig. 2: Add pennies or other small coins to each can.

Safety Tips and Setup Hints

(Continued from page 52)

- Once you have put the objects into the cans, cover the mouth of the can with masking tape or duct tape so the pennies do not fall out when you turn the can over.

- Because the exact weight of a can of liquid will depend on the type of liquid in the can and the type and amount of metal used in the can, we will pretend the weight of one can is 12 ounces (340 g).

Credit: The original idea for this lab was published in *Look to the Sky*, by Jerry DeBruin and Don Murad (Good Apple, 1988).

Step 3: Challenge friends and family to guess which can goes with which world. Have the unopened "Earth" can available for them to lift and compare with their guesses. Turn the can over to show the label when each person makes a guess. You can give the challenges in any order, but here is a suggestion (Fig. 3):

Planet with strongest gravity	The heaviest can	Jupiter
Two rocky planets with gravity about one-third that of Earth	The two cans that weigh about one-third what the Earth can weighs	Mercury, Mars
Two planets with gravity just slightly less than Earth	The two cans that weigh a little less than what the Earth can weighs	Venus, Uranus
Two giant planets	The two cans that weigh a little more than what the Earth can weighs	Saturn, Neptune
Two moons	The two cans that weigh about one-sixth what the Earth can weighs	Moon, Io
Two dwarf planets	The two cans that weigh the least	Ceres, Pluto

Fig. 3: Lift each can and compare the weights to the Earth can.

☀ Creative Enrichment

If you took a 12-ounce (340 g) can of soda to the Sun, it would weigh 27 times more, or about 20 pounds (9 kg). Can you find something around the house that weighs about 20 pounds (9 kg) to represent the weight of a can of soda on the Sun?

Walking to the Rocky Planets

Time

30 minutes

Materials

- 20 to 25 sheets of white copy paper
- Permanent marker
- Clear or masking tape
- Tape measure at least 3 feet (1 m) long
- 1 piece of string just over 18 inches (26 cm) long
- Scissors
- 1 container of play dough or play clay
- Small ruler that shows centimeters and millimeters

Safety Tips and Setup Hints

- Tape the sheets of copy paper together edge to edge to make a square at least 36 inches (92 cm) on a side.
- Tape the piece of string to the marker so the distance between the free end of the string and the marker is 18 inches (26 cm). Tape the free end of the string to the middle of the square. Stretch out the string so you

(Continues on page 58)

You don't need a spaceship to go from planet to planet. Just grab your walking shoes.

Instructions

Step 1: Place the Sun at one end of your model. (Fig. 1)

Step 2: Walk the following number of steps for each planet at the right distance scale (remember to make your steps about 2 feet (60 cm) apart). As you get to the spot for each planet, leave the sign and model there, and then move on to the next spot. (Fig. 2)

Planet orbit	Number of steps
Mercury	62 steps from the Sun
Venus	54 steps from Mercury
Earth	45 steps from Venus
Mars	84 steps from Earth

Step 3: When you get to Mars, look back at your model. The distances are amazing, right? (Fig. 3) ◆

(Continues on page 58)

Fig. 1: The paper circle represents our Sun.

Fig. 2: Count the number of steps
from planet to planet.

Safety Tips and Setup Hints

(Continued from page 56)

can draw a circle that is 36 inches (92 cm) in diameter. Cut out the circle. This will represent the Sun in our scale model.

- Use the play dough to make models of the rocky planets. Use the small ruler to measure the diameter of the balls of clay. Use the millimeter scale on the ruler rather than inches: Mercury (3 millimeters), Venus (8 millimeters), Earth (a little bigger than 8 millimeters), Mars (a little more than 4 millimeters). You may want to glue or tape each clay model to the sign for each planet so it does not get lost.

- To do this lab at this scale, you will need an open field or a sidewalk 500 feet (153 m) long. When you are walking the right number of steps from the Sun for each planet model, try to make your steps about 2 feet (60 cm) apart (you may want to practice doing this with a ruler or tape measure so you can get it right before you go out to make your model).

Creative Enrichment

Make a scale model showing planet sizes, distances, PLUS positions, all to scale. Find out where the planets should be using the website mentioned in "The Science Behind the Fun" (at right), and match your walking model and your planet model positions to these locations. You can also change the year, month, and day to show what the planet positions looked like on another day. Try today's planet positions, or even your birthday!

Fig. 3: Wow, the planets are far apart!

The Science Behind the Fun

Look at a picture that includes all the planets in our Solar System. Many times, the picture might have the planets scaled to size, meaning the sizes of the planets are to scale with one another, but the distances between them on the page are not correct. Or, if you look at a picture of the planets with correct distances, the planets would be so small they would be the size of specks of dust—or smaller! It is not easy to show planets and other objects scaled to size AND distance. This is the reason behind a walking scale model. With this sort of a model, you can see the sizes of planets and other objects to scale with the distances between them. Now that you see the model, does it make sense that it takes months and years for our spacecraft to go from one place to another?

One problem, even with walking scale models, is they make the planets appear always to be in a straight line. In reality, the planets move around the Sun at different speeds and they are almost always NOT in a line. Can you make a scale model where the planets are in their correct locations AND scaled to size AND scaled to distance? Yes! To do this, you will need to know where the planets are on a particular date. To find the positions of the planets today, use this website: www.fourmilab.ch/cgi-bin/Solar. Use these details for the scale:

Time = Now

Show = Images

Display = Inner System

Size = 900

Orbits = Real

Once you have entered these details, click "Update."

Walking to the Edge of the Solar System

Time
30 minutes

Materials

- 1 sign for each of the following worlds: Sun, Mercury, Venus, Earth, Mars, Jupiter, Saturn, Uranus, Neptune, Pluto, Eris, and Edge of the Solar System
- 2 signs for the Asteroid Belt
- Tape measure

Safety Tips and Setup Hints

- To do this lab at this scale, you will need an open field or a stretch of sidewalk 250 feet (76 m) long. When you are walking the right number of steps from the Sun for each planet, try to make your steps about 2 feet (60 cm) apart.

How far away is the edge of our Solar System? It's far. Really far!

Instructions

Step 1: Place the Sun sign at one end of your model. (Fig. 1)

Step 2: Place the signs for Mercury, Venus, Earth, and Mars at the correct distances from the Sun using the tape measure. Mercury should be 10 inches (25 cm) from the sign for the Sun. Venus should be 20 inches (50 cm) from the Sun. Earth will be placed 27 inches (68 cm) from the Sun, and Mars should be 41 inches (103 cm) from the Sun. (Fig. 2)

Step 3: For the rest of the model, walk the following number of steps (Fig. 3):

Location	Number of steps
Asteroid Belt	1 sign placed ½ step from Mars, 1 sign placed 2 steps from Mars
Jupiter	4 steps from Mars
Saturn	4 steps from Jupiter
Uranus	10 steps from Saturn
Neptune	11 steps from Uranus
Pluto (dwarf planet)	9 steps from Neptune
Eris (dwarf planet)	28 steps from Pluto
Edge of the Solar System	58 steps from Eris

Fig. 3: Count the number of steps from one world to another.

Fig. 1: Put the Sun down first.

Fig. 2: Measure the distances from the Sun to the first four planets.

The Science Behind the Fun

This scale model is smaller than the one you created in Lab 18, "Walking to the Rocky Planets" (see page 56). If we did not make the model smaller, this model using that same scale would be enormous. While you could include the models you used in Lab 18, to get the distances between them right, you would need about 18,000 steps for your model to reach from the Sun to the edge of our Solar System. That's more than 6 miles (10 km)! Wow!

The distance between the Sun and the Earth is also given another name, an *astronomical unit*. Because distances between objects in our Solar System are so large, the numbers get very big very quickly. Referring to distances in astronomical units keeps us from having to write so many zeros!

Can you add in the speed of a light beam to your scale model? On this scale, a beam of light would take a little over eight minutes to travel from the Sun to the Earth, so you would need to take one step in about eight minutes. How long would it take for your light beam to travel to the rest of the locations in our model? *Hint: Multiply each step by 8.3 minutes.* The *Voyager 1* spacecraft is at the edge of our Solar System. About how long does it take for a signal to get from *Voyager 1* to us?

Creative Enrichment

The *Voyager 1* spacecraft is out near the edge of our Solar System. *Voyager 1* and *Voyager 2* both carry specially recorded pictures, sounds, and messages on a Golden Record in case an alien civilization ever found the spacecraft and wanted to learn about the beings who launched them. You can read about the Golden Record on the *Voyager* mission website: voyager.jpl.nasa.gov/spacecraft/goldenrec.html.

What would you put on a Golden Record if you wanted aliens to learn about you, your family, and Earth? Design your own and display it!

Walking through Another Solar System

Time

30 minutes

Materials

- The planet models, signs, and Sun paper model used in Lab 18, "Walking to the Rocky Planets" (see page 56)
- 1 additional container of play dough or play clay
- White copy paper
- Tape or glue
- Marker
- Small ruler that shows millimeters

Safety Tips and Setup Hints

- When you are walking the right number of steps for each planet, try to make your steps about 2 feet (60 cm) apart.
- Make five play dough balls in these sizes and attach them to pieces of paper with these labels:
    - 10 millimeters, labeled **Kepler-62b**
    - 5 millimeters, labeled **Kepler-62c**
    - 16 millimeters, labeled **Kepler-62d**
    - 13 millimeters, labeled **Kepler-62e**
    - 11 millimeters, labeled **Kepler-62f**

If you think we are limited to making scale models only of our own Solar System, think again!

Instructions

Step 1: Place the Sun at one end of your model. Set up Mercury, Venus, Earth, and Mars in a line at the same distances as you did in Lab 18, "Walking to the Rocky Planets" (see page 56). (Fig. 1)

Step 2: The other planet system will be compared to the size of our inner Solar System, and our Sun will stand in for the Kepler-62 star. Alongside the rocky planets, walk the following number of steps from the Sun for the Kepler-62 planets, and set up the models at each of the stops (Fig. 2):

Planet orbit	Number of steps
Kepler-62b	9 steps from the Sun
Kepler-62c	6 steps from Kepler-62b
Kepler-62d	4 steps from Kepler-62c
Kepler-62e	49 steps from Kepler-62d
Kepler-62f	47 steps from Kepler-62e

Step 3: Look back at your model. What do you notice about the Kepler-62 planet system? How does it compare to our inner Solar System? (Fig. 3) ✦

Fig. 1: Set up our inner Solar System.

Fig. 3: You can study two planet systems at the same time!

Creative Enrichment

Imagine a planet around another star. Is it a rocky world? A water world? An icy world? Is it a hot planet? Or maybe a cold planet? Identify what your planet is like. Then, imagine a kind of life form that could live on your planet. Draw what it would look like, and don't forget to draw your planet, too!

Fig. 2: Set up the Kepler-62 planet system.

The Science Behind the Fun

Before 1995, the only planets we knew of that orbited a star were the planets that go around our star, the Sun. In October 1995 scientists announced the discovery of the first planet orbiting another star. Planets that orbit other stars are called "exoplanets." Many telescopes have been used to discover many exoplanets—several thousand planets, in fact! The spacecraft that has been used to discover the most planets is called *Kepler*.

The *Kepler* spacecraft stared at the same part of the sky for just over four years and watched more than one hundred thousand stars at the same time. What scientists looked for was the light from a star dimming a tiny bit as a planet passed in front of that star blocking a small amount of its light. What is it called when a planet passes in front of a star? We learned this in Lab 8, "Eclipse the Sun, Eclipse the Moon" (see page 30): It's a transit!

What have we learned about other solar systems? They are all different! Some have many planets, and some have only one or two. Some planets are bigger than Jupiter, and some are smaller than Earth. Some planets go around their stars in about the same amount of time as Earth goes around the Sun, but some planets orbit their stars so fast that one year on these planets is equal to only a few Earth days!

To Andromeda!

Time
10 minutes

Materials
- 2 cookies, plus 1 of the same type of cookie for each person who will participate in the lab
- Tape measure at least 4 feet (1.2 m) in length
- Calculator

Safety Tips and Setup Hints
- This lab only requires two people to do, but it is even more fun if more people participate. Gather some family members! Give every person who joins in a cookie.
- Use a room with open floor space for this lab.

Think we are limited to making scale models of solar systems? Nope!

Instructions

Step 1: Hold one cookie in one hand, show it to the other lab participants, and identify it as a model of the Milky Way galaxy. Hold another cookie in your other hand, show it to everyone, and identify it as a model of the Andromeda galaxy. (Fig. 1)

Step 2: Give all other participants a cookie to hold. Put the cookie representing the Milky Way on a table or chair so everyone can see it.

Step 3: Invite participants to guess how far the Andromeda galaxy is from the Milky Way galaxy, if each was shrunk to the size of a cookie. Have each person stand with their model cookie as far from the Milky Way cookie as they feel the Andromeda galaxy is from the Milky Way galaxy on this scale. (Fig. 2)

Step 4: Once everyone has made their guesses, the size of the scale model will depend on the size of the cookie you chose for your model. Measure the diameter of a cookie. Using the calculator, multiply the diameter of the cookie (in inches or cm) by 25. For example, a 1-inch (2.5 cm) wide Andromeda galaxy cookie would be placed 25 inches (63 cm) from the Milky Way cookie. Place the Andromeda galaxy cookie at the right distance from the Milky Way cookie. How did everyone else's guesses compare to the real scale? ◆

Fig. 1: The Milky Way and Andromeda galaxies shrunk to cookie size!

Creative Enrichment

The Hubble Space Telescope has taken pictures of lots of different galaxies. You can see many of them on a gallery on the Hubble website: hubblesite.org/gallery/album/galaxy. Look at all the different shapes. How would you sort these galaxies? If you can, print out the gallery pages and cut out the pictures. If you cannot print the pictures, grab crayons or colored pencils and sketch some of your favorites. Create a way to display the ways you have sorted your galaxies. Invite family members to sort some galaxies, too!

The Science Behind the Fun

In earlier activities, we explored the Sun, the Moon, planets, and solar systems. But what is a galaxy? A galaxy is a huge collection of stars, solar systems, and other things, all held together by gravity. Some only contain a few hundred thousand stars, while others contain over 1 trillion stars. Our Milky Way galaxy contains over 200,000,000,000, or *200 billion*, stars.

Galaxies come in different shapes. Some, such as our Milky Way galaxy, are spiral- or pinwheel-shaped. Others, called "elliptical" galaxies, are shaped like a ball. Still others, called "irregular" galaxies, have no shape.

Were you surprised by the size of this scale model? Was it smaller than you imagined? We often think of the distances between galaxies as huge, and, while they really are big distances, the distances between galaxies compared to the sizes of the galaxies can be surprisingly small.

How far apart are the Milky Way and Andromeda galaxies? Astronomers have figured out the distance is about 2,500,000 light-years. But what is a light-year? A beam of light travels about 186,000 miles (300,000 km) in one second, called a "light-second". Light travels close to 6 trillion miles (10 trillion km) in one year: a "light-year".

The Milky Way galaxy is about 100,000 light-years from one side to another. How many miles is this? It is close to 600,000,000,000,000,000! And how far apart are the Milky Way and Andromeda galaxies in miles? About 15,000,000,000,000,000,000! Now do you see why astronomers use light-years to describe distances?

Fig. 2: How far is the Andromeda galaxy from the Milky Way galaxy? Guess!

Everything Is Moving Away!

Time

10 minutes

Materials

- 1 round 12-inch (30 cm) balloon
- Permanent marker
- 1 piece of string about 12 inches (30 cm) long
- Ruler
- Binder clip or clothespin
- Your science notebook
- Pencil

Safety Tips and Setup Hints

- Blow four medium breaths into the balloon, fold over or twist the nozzle, and hold it closed using the clip. Make sure no air escapes. You may need to practice doing this until you can keep the air in the balloon.

- Take the marker and draw a small dot somewhere on the balloon. Label it "MW" so you can identify it later. This will represent our home galaxy, the Milky Way.

- Draw another dot a few inches or centimeters away. Label this dot with a small number 1. Draw

(Continues on page 68)

When we look out at faraway galaxies in the Universe, they are all moving away from us. What does that look like?

Instructions

Step 1: Put one end of the piece of string at the MW dot. Stretch the string out to the dot labeled "1." Be careful you do not press into the balloon. Just gently lay the string across the balloon from the MW dot to the 1 dot. Be careful not to let the string slide around too much. Pinch the string where the 1 dot is. (Fig. 1)

Step 2: Without losing where you pinched the string, lay the string next to the ruler. Measure the length from the end of the string to where you pinched it using inches or centimeters as carefully as you can. (Fig. 2)

Step 3: Record the length from the MW dot to the 1 dot in your science notebook. If you used the rows and columns, you would write this in the 1 row under the "First Measurement" column. (Fig. 3)

Step 4: Repeat these measurements for the rest of the dots, measuring from the MW dot and recording each length in your notebook in the "First Measurement" column.

Step 5: Very carefully, undo the clip holding the balloon closed. Do not let *any* air out of the balloon. If you do, you will have to start over and redo all your measurements. Blow three or four more medium breaths into the balloon. Do not let it pop. Twist and clip the balloon closed. (Fig. 4)

(Continues on page 68)

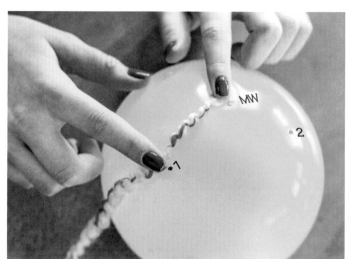

Fig. 1: Stretch your string from MW to 1.

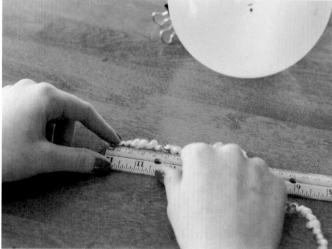

Fig. 2: Measure the string.

Fig. 3: Write your measurement in your notebook.

Fig. 4: Blow more air into your balloon.

Safety Tips and Setup Hints

(Continued from page 66)

nine more dots on the balloon. Scatter them unevenly, and make sure they are a few inches or centimeters apart from each other, not all bunched into one spot. Number each dot. You should have one MW dot and dots numbered 1 through 9 when you are finished.

- Here is one way you can record your science data for this lab: Make a table in your science notebook that has ten rows and three columns. In the first row, label the columns "Dot," "First Measurement," and "Second Measurement." In the first column, "Dot," write 1 in the first box, 2 in the box under it, and so on, until you have filled all the boxes in the first column up to 9. Remember, if you find a way to record your data that works better for you, use it!

Step 6: Do the measurements again from the MW dot to the 1 dot, and so on. Record the data in your notebook in the "Second Measurement" column. (Fig. 5)

Step 7: Look at your data. What do you notice about the distances from the MW dot to the rest of the dots from the first measurements to the second?

Creative Enrichment

Repeat the same lab all over again, but this time, do all the measurements from the 1 dot. Blow four breaths into the balloon. Measure from the 1 dot to the MW dot, then from the 1 dot to the 2 dot, and so on. Blow two to four more breaths into the balloon. Do the measurements again. What do you notice? Are you still not sure? Then do it again, this time using the 2 dot, or the 5 dot, or any of the other dots. What do you see?

Fig. 5: Do your measurements again.

The Science Behind the Fun

Centuries ago, people thought the Earth was at the center of the Universe. It made sense that they thought like this. If you go outside, you don't notice the Earth is spinning. It *looks* like everything is going around the Earth, doesn't it? Then came Polish astronomer Nicolaus Copernicus. He used math to figure out that the Earth was not at the center of the Universe and that our planet actually orbited the Sun. Later, Galileo used his telescope to show evidence that this was true. For the next three hundred years our telescopes got better, and astronomers learned a lot about the stars in our Milky Way galaxy. Until the 1920s, though, astronomers thought the Milky Way galaxy contained all the stars in the whole Universe.

In 1925 astronomer Edwin Hubble showed that some of the "nebulae" (NEB-you-lee) or "gas clouds" they could see were, in fact, other faraway galaxies. Astronomers proved that very faraway galaxies were moving away from our Milky Way! But, does this mean our Milky Way is the center of the Universe? Nope! What is amazing is that no matter which galaxy you are in, distant galaxies look like they are expanding away from you because the Universe itself is expanding. Does this seem difficult to think about? Test this idea using the Creative Enrichment activity!

Light, Motion, Gravity

How many places have people been to in our Solar System? So far, just two places—the Earth and our Moon. How many places have our spacecraft been to in our Solar System? We have sent our unmanned spacecraft to all the planets and many of the moons of those planets, plus the dwarf planets Pluto and Ceres, plus a few comets and asteroids.

It is definitely easier to learn more about something if you can get closer to it. If our spacecraft go to a planet, such as Mars, we can see details on its surface and we can study its atmosphere. We can see how Mars changes over the course of days, months, or years. We learn a lot that way!

The farthest that one of our spacecraft has been is past the edge of our Solar System. In terms of the size of our whole Milky Way galaxy, though, this is just a quick little hop. Distances between things in our Milky Way are *huge*, and distances between galaxies are even *bigger*!

So, how do we learn about things in space if we can't send a spacecraft there? Everything we know about things in the Universe we can learn using light, motion, and gravity. Light carries information that tells us what something is made of and what is going on there. The motion of things we can see can tell us about things we cannot see. Gravity pulls things together. These are the tools we use to learn about places we can't touch!

How do we know what this gas cloud, called the Orion Nebula, is made of? The different kinds of light coming from it tell us!

Credit: NASA, ESA, M. Robberto (Space Telescope Science Institute/ESA), and the Hubble Space Telescope Orion Treasury Project Team

LAB 23

The Colors in Light

Time

15 minutes

Materials

- 1 compact disc, such as a music CD
- 1 piece of white copy paper (optional)
- Camera, or colored pencils or crayons
- Your science notebook
- Pencil
- 1 clear drinking glass (try one made of clear glass first)
- Water

Safety Tips and Setup Hints

- **Never look directly at the Sun,** and do not reflect the Sun's light into your eyes or anyone else's eyes. Doing so may *very quickly* cause eye damage or blindness.
- It is best to do this lab on a sunny day.

This lab includes two different ways to see the colors in light. Try them both!

Instructions

Step 1: For the first activity, take the CD out of its packaging.

Step 2: Go to a window where sunlight is coming in through the window. Put the CD into the beam of sunlight, and angle the CD until you see colors on a nearby wall or the floor. Move the CD around to make the colors as bright as possible. If the wall or the floor is dark, try using a white piece of paper as a screen. (Fig. 1)

Step 3: To record what you see, take a picture of the colors, and put the picture in your science notebook. If you do not have a camera, use colored pencils or crayons to draw the shades of color onto the white paper screen. (You may need a second person to hold the CD steady for you while you color.) (Fig. 2)

Step 4: For the second activity, fill the clear drinking glass mostly full of water, and take it over to the sunny window. Angle the glass around (careful not to spill!) until you see colors on the wall or floor. Record them as you did the colors you saw with the CD. (Fig. 3) ◆

Fig. 1: Reflect the Sun's light off the CD.

Fig. 2: Record the colors you see.

Creative Enrichment

There are many ways you can make a spectrum. See which combination of prism and light source works best. Try different shapes of drinking glasses, try clear glass versus clear plastic, or use different colors of glasses. See if your school science lab has a glass prism you can borrow. Try different light sources, such as flashlights, LED lights, candle flames, bright lightbulbs, or any other kind of light you have around the house. See if using a darkened room helps you see the colors more easily, or try making the beam of sunlight smaller by closing shades or blinds. Which combination worked best? Were the colors the same for each light source? Were any colors brighter than others?

Be especially careful with candles and flames! Have an adult around to help.

Fig. 3: Hold a glass of water in sunlight.

The Science Behind the Fun

Have you ever noticed a rainbow in the sky after a rainstorm? Or maybe you have seen a little rainbow on a sunny day when you look in the misty spray from a garden hose? Where do these rainbows come from? The light source in both of these cases is the Sun. But what makes the rainbow?

The light from the Sun looks like it is all the same. We call light from the Sun "white light." White light from the Sun is actually made up of lots of different colors. You used the glass filled with water and the CD to split the white light into those colors. The array of colors you see is called the "spectrum." The water and glass bent, or "refracted," the white light, and the different colors bent at different angles, so the colors spread out into a rainbow. A tool that spreads light out like this is called a "prism." A rainbow in the sky or from a garden hose forms when tiny drops of water act like little prisms, and they spread light out into the rainbow you see. The CD works because all the thousands of tiny tracks on the CD act like little prisms.

You probably saw many different shades of color. While the colors of the rainbow are often listed as red, orange, yellow, green, blue, indigo, and violet, in fact, all the colors we can see are in the spectrum, not just those colors. There aren't sharp bands of color, like some people draw rainbows. In the 1660s and 1670s, scientist Sir Isaac Newton was the first person to figure out how prisms and rainbows actually worked.

Why Is the Sky Blue?

It's a question *ALL* have asked. Let's find the answer!

Fig. 1: Make a glass of milky water.

Instructions

Step 1: Fill the glass or bowl with water until it is mostly full.

Step 2: Put a few drops of milk into the water, and stir the water with the spoon. You can use an eyedropper for this, but, if you do not have one, just carefully and slowly pour a few drops of milk from a spoon into the water. Do not pour the milk directly from the carton, as it will likely come out too quickly. Put a little bit of milk into a small bowl, and scoop a few drops into a spoon, then into the water. (Fig. 1)

Step 3: Shine the flashlight through the water. What color do you see? (The color will be fairly light.) (Fig. 2)

The Science Behind the Fun

Earth's air is made of several gases. Most of it is nitrogen, about 78 percent, about 21 percent is oxygen, there is a little bit of a gas called argon, a little water vapor, and very small amounts of gases, such as carbon dioxide and others. While our eyes can't see the individual bits of gases, called "atoms" or "molecules," we can feel them when the wind blows. The amounts of these gases change depending on the seasons, the altitude, the weather, whether there has been a volcanic eruption, or other reasons, but these are generally the amounts we measure.

As we learned in Lab 23, "The Colors in Light" (see page 72), the light from the Sun is made of many colors, and we can see those colors when we split the Sun's white light using a prism. When white light hits the gas molecules, most of the light—such as the reds, oranges, and yellows—is able to move its way through the molecules and pass to the ground to your eyes. However, the blue light is scattered around by the gases. It is this scattered blue light we see as a blue sky. In this lab, the big particles of milk in the water acted like the particles of air, scattering the blue light from the flashlight. You can try playing with the amount of milk in the water and the type of flashlight until you get the easiest blue color to see.

Remember Lab 6, "Our Colorful Sun" (see page 24)? We learned there why our Sun appears yellow—because the blue light from the Sun is scattered, leaving our Sun looking more yellow than it really is. Now you know why and how the light is scattered!

Creative Enrichment

Is our sky always the exact same color of blue? Go to a local hardware store and pick up many different shades of blue paint color sample cards. You may have to get sample cards from several different paint manufacturers to get a good range of colors. Make a holder for those samples, and keep track of the blue color in the sky from day to day, or week to week. If you travel to another city or state, take your color sample cards with you, and see what the blue color is like there. Keep track of weather conditions like temperature and humidity to see if you can find a relationship between the color and what is happening in our air. If you know someone who lives in a different place, do the same lab together at the same time on the same day. Do you both see the exact same color?

Mixing Light to Make Color

Time
10 minutes

Materials

- Rimmed baking (or "cookie") sheet
- Waxed paper
- 1 package of red, green, blue, and yellow liquid food coloring
- 1 fork
- Several toothpicks
- 3 large clear glass drinking glasses
- Water
- 1 spoon
- 3 bright flashlights
- Your science notebook
- Pencil

Safety Tips and Setup Hints

- It is best to use three flash-lights that are all the same brightness level. If your flashlights can't be focused, try wrapping the front of the flashlight with an aluminum foil collar a few inches wide.

(Continues on page 78)

Red, blue, and yellow are the primary colors of paint, but what are the primary colors of light?

Instructions

Step 1: Put three drops of red food coloring on the sheet a few inches (centimeters) apart. Add one drop of green to one drop of red; put one drop of blue into the second red drop, and put one drop of yellow into the third.

Next, put two drops of green on the sheet. Put one drop of blue into one, and put one drop of yellow into the second.

Next, put one drop of blue onto the sheet and put one drop of yellow into it.

Finally, combine one drop each of red, blue, and yellow. Use a fork (wipe it off between drops) or toothpicks to combine each set of drops. Don't forget to label each set so you can remember which colors went into them. What colors do you see? (If your food coloring is really concentrated, try dipping toothpicks into the mixture to see the colors, or put the drops of coloring into small glasses of water.) (Fig. 1)

Step 2: Next, fill each large glass with an equal amount of water. Now, put a few drops of red into one glass, a few drops of blue into another glass, and a few drops of green into the third glass. Make the colors bright. Stir each glass with the spoon, but be sure to clean your spoon each time before you put it into a glass so you don't mix up the colors! (Fig. 2)

(Continues on page 78)

Fig. 1: Mix drops of food coloring.

Fig. 2: Put drops of food coloring into glasses.

The Science Behind the Fun

The primary colors of paint (pigment) are red, blue, and yellow. The word *primary* means these colors can't be made by mixing other colors. When you need to make more colors than these three, you would combine those colors to make other colors:

yellow + blue = green

yellow + red = orange

blue + red = purple

If you combine red, blue, and yellow pigment, you get black.

The primary colors of light are different: red, green, and blue. When you combine the primary colors of light, you get other colors, but these are different from the combinations of pigments.

red + green = yellow

red + blue = magenta (a kind of purple)

blue + green = cyan (a kind of light blue)

If you stand really close to a television set, you might see tiny dots of color. The TV picture is made from millions of these little dots, and each dot is a separate red, blue, or green light that can be switched on or off very quickly. If you combine red, green, and blue light, you get white light.

(Continues on page 79)

Safety Tips and Setup Hints

(Continued from page 76)

- Use a room that can be darkened.

- Be careful with food coloring. It can stain clothes, skin, and furniture.

- Tear off a sheet of waxed paper and put it on the baking sheet. The edges of the baking sheet will keep drops from spilling, and the waxed paper will keep the drops from rolling around too much.

Step 3: Shine one flashlight sideways through the red glass onto a white wall or piece of paper. Shine another flashlight through the green glass. Shine the third flashlight through the blue glass. (Fig. 3)

Step 4: Move the flashlights around so you can combine the light from the red and green glasses. What color do you see on the wall beyond? Then, combine the light from the red and blue glasses. Next, combine the light from the blue and green glasses. What colors do you see each time you do this? Finally, combine the red, green, and blue light together. What do you see? (Fig. 4)

Fig. 4: Mix colors of light. What do you see?

Fig. 3: Splash color onto the wall using flashlights.

The Science Behind the Fun

(Continued from page 77)

By the 1600s, some scientists thought different colors of light were due to a combination
of light and darkness. The idea was that red
light was white light that had a little darkness added, and blue had the most darkness
added. In the late 1600s, Isaac Newton used
a prism and split white light into its colors.
He then combined the colors again and
produced—you guessed it—white light! He
proved the prior idea to be wrong.

Creative Enrichment

There are so many combinations you can
make for colors of pigment and colors of
light! In this lab, you used one drop of each
color of food coloring, but what happens if
you add different numbers of drops, such as
one red drop + two blue drops + three yellow
drops? You can also make many different
combinations of colors of light. Try adding
drops of two different colors to each glass of
water, then combining the light from each
glass. Or, try adding more drops of one color
to each glass to make a darker color, or add
more water to make a lighter color. Then,
shine the flashlights through the glasses like
you did before. Make as many combinations
of pigment and light as you can think of—and
be sure to keep track of your experiments in
your notebook. What do you see?

Time

10 minutes

Materials

- Clear kitchen plastic wrap
- Bright flashlight
- Black permanent marker
- 1 set of colored permanent markers
- Rubber band
- 4 to 5 small colored objects

Safety Tips and Setup Hints

- You will need some small colored objects you can hold. For example, you could use a red apple, a yellow tennis ball, an orange, a green leaf, a blue piece of cloth, a purple flower ... or use your imagination! Just grab at least four or five objects.

- The set of permanent markers should at least have red, green, and blue, but if you have more colors, that's even better!

Does a red object always look red? Shine a light on this question!

Instructions

Step 1: Tear off a sheet of plastic wrap big enough to wrap around the bulb end of your flashlight. Turn the bulb end of the flashlight over and place it on the plastic wrap. Make sure the plastic is flat with no wrinkles. Use the black marker to draw a circle around the bulb end of the flashlight. (Fig. 1)

Step 2: Take a red permanent marker, and color inside the black circle evenly. Put the red circle at the light end of the flashlight, wrap the edges of the plastic around the end of the flashlight, and wrap the rubber band around the flashlight to hold the plastic in place. Turn on the flashlight to make sure you can see red light. Do the same steps for each of the colored markers. (Fig. 2)

Step 3: Line up your colored objects in a row. Put the red plastic over the flashlight and turn it on. Turn off the room lights. (Fig. 3)

Step 4: Shine the red light slowly along the row of objects. Which object looks brightest in the red light? Which object looks darkest in red light? (Fig. 4)

Step 5: Replace the red plastic with another color and shine the light along the row of objects again. Which object looks brightest or darkest? Do the same for all your marker colors. When do you notice that the color of the object is brightest? When is the object darkest? ◆

Fig. 1: Outline a black circle around the flashlight.

Fig. 2: Make plastic circles for each colored marker.

Fig. 3: Get your objects and red light ready.

Fig. 4: Shine the red light on all your objects.

Creative Enrichment

Develop a light and color fashion show in a dark room with your different colors of light and different colored pieces of clothing. Don't let your audience see each piece of clothing before you start. Have your audience guess the colors in each of your pieces of clothing as you shine different colors of light on them, and then turn the white light on to reveal their colors!

The Science Behind the Fun

A red apple always looks red, right? Well, not exactly. When you shine a regular flashlight onto a red apple, it looks red. Why does it look red, though? Remember that light coming from a regular flashlight, a lamp, or the Sun is called "white light." White light is made of all colors. The red apple reflects red light to your eyes, and it absorbs all the other colors of light. A blue shirt reflects blue light to your eyes, and it absorbs all the other colors of light. A white wall reflects all the colors of light, so it appears white, whereas a black piece of paper absorbs all the colors of light and reflects none of them.

As we learned in Lab 25, "Mixing Light to Make Color" (see page 76), Isaac Newton helped us learn a lot about light and color. One other thing he did in his experiments was to shine sunlight, or white light, through a prism and separate the colors. He then pointed one of those colors of light toward different objects. Newton saw that no matter what he did, that color of light remained the same color. He figured out the colors of objects had to do with the light shining on them.

Detecting Infrared Light

Time

15 minutes

Materials

- Flat black paint or black permanent marker
- Alcohol thermometer
- Cardboard box
- Scissors or box cutter
- Glass prism
- 1 sheet of white copy paper
- Watch or timer

Safety Tips and Setup Hints

- Alcohol thermometers look like they have red-colored water in the bulb.
- Color the bulb of the thermometer with flat (not shiny) black paint or black permanent marker. Black paint works best, but if you do not have it, black marker will do. Let the paint or marker dry completely before you start.
- If your box has flaps on top, have an adult cut them off with the scissors or box cutter.

Use simple materials to detect something you can't see!

Instructions

Step 1: Cut a notch out of the top of one side of the box just big enough to hold the prism. You want the sides of the notch to hold the prism without you holding the prism with your hands. Put the prism into the notch. (Fig. 1)

Step 2: Put the sheet of paper on the bottom of the box. (Fig. 2)

Step 3: Go outside on a sunny day around noon or 1 p.m. in late spring, summer, or early autumn. Find a spot in the sun but out of the wind. Bring the box, the prism, thermometer, and timer. Turn the prism slowly until you see a rainbow on the bottom of the box. You may need to turn the box around to get the rainbow to appear on the bottom of the box. (Fig. 3)

Step 4: Put the thermometer somewhere nearby in the shade. Let it sit for a few minutes. Record the temperature on the thermometer.

Step 5: Look at the rainbow and see where the red end is. Put the thermometer just off the red end where it looks like there is no color. (Fig. 4)

Step 6: Let the thermometer sit in that part of the box for five to fifteen minutes (you may need to adjust the position of the box slightly to keep the rainbow in place, but do not let any of the rainbow touch the thermometer). At the end of the time, note the temperature on the thermometer again. What do you notice? ✦

Fig. 1: Slide the prism into the notch in the box.

Fig. 2: Put the paper in the box.

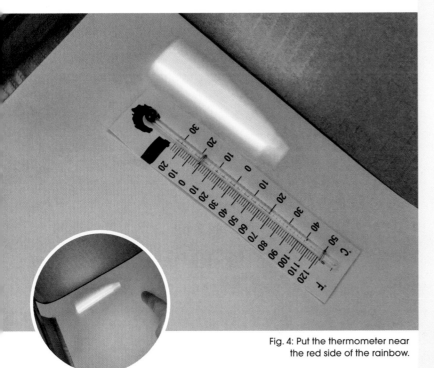

Fig. 3: Look for a rainbow in the box.

Fig. 4: Put the thermometer near the red side of the rainbow.

The Science Behind the Fun

In 1800 astronomer William Herschel was experimenting with the light from the Sun passing through his prism, and he noticed his thermometer recorded the highest temperature when it wasn't actually in the rainbow itself. The highest temperature he saw was just off the red end of the rainbow. He had discovered a form of light he couldn't see with his eyes. This light was called "infrared" (IN-fruh-RED). "Infra" in Latin means "below," so this was a form of light below the red end of the rainbow.

Infrared light is extremely useful. Infrared cameras are used to locate people and animals caught in thick smoke and for finding areas of forest that have burned where it looks like the fire is out, but are actually still hot enough to flare up and burn again. Infrared cameras are used to see where heat is escaping from buildings and wasting energy. Infrared telescopes see hidden things in space, too. Visible light cannot pass through dark dusty areas in space, but infrared light can, allowing us to see those stars that are normally hidden.

Creative Enrichment

This lab works best around midday, especially when the Sun is high in the sky. What happens to your results when you do this experiment early or late in the day? How about when the Sun is lower in the sky in early spring, late fall, or winter?

Can You See the Light?

Time

5 minutes

Materials

- Any handheld remote controls from around the house (TV, stereo, computer, and so forth)
- Phone camera or handheld camera
- Piece of dark plastic, such as a black plastic shopping bag or garbage bag

Safety Tips and Setup Hints

- It helps to do this lab in a darkened room.
- If you are using a phone camera and there are two cameras on the phone, try using both cameras. This may work better in one of the cameras.

Use a camera to help you see the light.

Instructions

Step 1: Grab a few remote controls. Look at the front of one of the remote controls. Press and hold a button. Do you see anything happening on the front of the remote? (Fig. 1)

Step 2: Turn on the camera. Point the front of a remote control at the camera. Press and hold a button on the remote control. Look at the image on the screen as you press the button. Now, do you see anything on the screen? Try switching the camera to the backward-facing camera and press the button again. Try this with a few different remotes. (Fig. 2)

Step 3: Now, put the remote into the black plastic bag. Point the front of the remote toward the camera and press a button. What do you see in the camera? (Fig. 3)

Fig. 2: Look at the remote using the camera.

Fig. 1: Press a button on the remote. Do you see anything?

Fig. 3: Can you see anything through the plastic bag?

The Science Behind the Fun

Did you notice you couldn't see anything on the front of the remote when you pressed a button, but you could when you pointed the remote at the camera? How about when you put the remote into the plastic bag? You definitely couldn't see through the bag, but you saw light coming from the front of the remote. What was going on there? Doesn't a camera see the same kind of light our eyes can see?

Well, not exactly. Our eyes see a certain kind of energy called "visible light." There are other kinds of energy, such as radio waves, microwaves, ultraviolet rays, X-rays, and gamma rays. And, there is another kind called "infrared" waves. Remote controls communicate with televisions and other electronics using infrared waves. Our eyes cannot normally see infrared waves, but our cameras can often see a little bit of infrared light, and this is what shows up when we point remote controls at our cameras.

The camera is able to take a form of light you cannot see and turn it into an image you can see. Astronomers do this, too! When they take a picture of something our eyes cannot see, they need to turn it into a picture you can see. For example, the Hubble Space Telescope can see visible light and a little bit of infrared light. Here are two pictures of the same dusty cloud in space, called the Eagle Nebula (NEB-you-luh).

The picture on the left shows us the nebula in visible light, and the picture on the right shows it to us in infrared light. The views are completely different! What do you notice in each image?

Creative Enrichment

Set up your camera in a darkened room so you can use the camera that shows you infrared light from your remotes the best and you do not have to hold the camera to see the view on the screen. You may need to prop the camera on a shelf or counter (or you may need a second person to hold the camera for you). Find several small objects from around the house. Practice "painting" an object with infrared light from the remote so that the remote shines its light on the object and you can see the object "light up" in the camera view. Move the remote so the light shines all over the object. Take a few videos while you "paint" different objects with infrared light. Have other people watch the videos and challenge them to guess the objects you are using just by seeing them in the videos. Give a prize for the person who guesses the most objects correctly!

Credit: NASA, ESA, and the Hubble Heritage Team (STScI/AURA)

Make and Bake

Time

1 to 2 hours

Materials

- Clean, empty pizza box (from a medium-size pizza)
- Scissors or box cutter
- Aluminum foil
- Duct tape or clear packing tape
- 1 heavy gallon-size (3.4 L) zip-top bag
- Black paper
- 5 or 6 sheets of newspaper
- Clear glass or plastic plate (not paper)
- Graham crackers, chocolate, and marshmallows (for s'mores)

Safety Tips and Setup Hints

- If you need a clean pizza box, ask your local pizza shop for an extra box the next time you order a pizza. Tell them it's for science!
- This lab works best on a sunny day with very little wind. If it is windy, try to block your solar oven from the wind because wind might cool it down.

Making s'mores requires no fire at all—just a sunny day.

Instructions

Step 1: Flip the top of the pizza box up, and have an adult cut along three sides of the top to make a flap. Leave a 1-inch (2.5 cm) border around the edge of the box top. (Fig. 1)

Step 2: Pull the flap up, cover the inside of the flap with aluminum foil, and tape the foil onto the back of the flap.

Step 3: Cut the sides of the zip-top bag apart so you have two pieces of clear plastic. Cover the inside of the opening you cut into the box top with a sheet of plastic. Tape all sides of the plastic to the lid so no air can get through the sides.

Step 4: Cover the bottom of the pizza box with black paper and tape it down along the edges or by adding tape to the back of the paper. (Fig. 2)

Step 5: Roll sheets of newspaper into tubes and place them on the bottom of the box all along the edges of the box. Make sure you can still close the lid of the box. If you can't, make the rolls a little smaller. (Fig. 3)

Step 6: Take your solar cooker outside into the sunlight, and put it on a hard surface. Angle the aluminum foil flap until sunlight is passing through the clear plastic top into the cooker. Use a piece of cardboard or something sturdy to hold the flap at the right angle. You may also want to prop the box so the foil points directly at the Sun. (Fig. 4)

Fig. 1: Cut a flap in the box top.

Creative Enrichment

Test your solar oven by placing a cooking thermometer inside it that can show temperatures up to 200°F (about 93°C). Let your oven sit in the Sun for an hour or two. How hot does it get? Can you think of ways to make your solar oven even better? Can you angle more sunlight into the oven, change the design to get a hotter temperature, or make your oven bigger? Try new designs and see what works best! Remember, don't use magnifying glasses or any lenses that might set the paper or cardboard on fire. That would be too hot—and too dangerous!

The Science Behind the Fun

How does light from the Sun end up as heat to cook food? First, sunlight enters the clear top of your cooker. The light hits the black paper at the bottom, and the black paper gives off heat that heats up the air inside the box. The plastic top and the rolled-up newspaper keep the hot air from escaping, and the temperature inside can heat up to 125°F (about 50°C) or even more. While it is true that solar cookers take a LONG while to heat up and cook food, they use completely free energy!

If you try other foods in your cooker, *don't use foods with raw eggs, mayonnaise, or raw meat.* Your cooker may not get hot enough to kill all the bad bacteria. Use meats that are already cooked, or vegetables or fruits. Try making baked peach slices with cinnamon and honey, baked hot dog pieces, or kale chips!

Solar ovens may be a great idea for areas of the world with no electricity. NASA also uses solar energy in a lot of ways, but especially to make electricity to power spacecraft and the International Space Station.

Step 7: Put the food you want to cook onto a clear plastic or clear glass plate. For example, put a graham cracker on the plate and the chocolate on top. Top another graham cracker with a marshmallow. Put the plate inside your cooker and let the food cook so the chocolate begins to melt. When your chocolate is melted, stick the two halves together—a s'more! Don't open your cooker too many times, or you will let the warm air out.

Fig. 2: Tape black paper inside the box.

Fig. 3: Put newspaper rolls inside the box.

Fig. 4: Shine sunlight into your cooker.

LAB 30

Shine a Little Light

Time

30 minutes

Materials

- Small mirrors (at least 6, but more is even better)
- 1 small object
- Flashlight

Safety Tips and Setup Hints

- If you need to buy mirrors, look for small flat plastic mirrors. Mirrors about 3 x 4 inches (7 x 10 cm) in size will be fine.
- Use a flashlight where the beam can be made smaller (usually by turning a ring around the light).
- If you do the Creative Enrichment "laser maze" lab, you will need a laser pointer. *Don't point the laser at anyone's eyes!*
- If you want to see the laser light, you can use a can of theater spray smoke. Be careful using the spray indoors. Make sure it is safe to use around smoke detectors. Sometimes it can leave a dusty film on surfaces, and some people may be allergic to the smoke material.

Make a maze of mirrors and invite friends and family to make your maze even better!

Fig. 1: Get your object ready.

Instructions

Step 1: Set up your object on one side of a long table or counter. (Fig. 1) Turn off the lights in the room.

Step 2: The goal is to set up as many mirrors as you can so when you shine the flashlight onto the first mirror, it shines onto the second, the third, and so on, until finally the light shines onto the object. You will need to prop your mirrors so they stand pretty much straight up. There is no one right answer for this. Set up your mirrors in any way you want. Make sure your light beam is as small as possible. (Fig. 2)

Step 3: Once you are really good at this, ask friends or family members to give it a try! Make it as difficult as you want. See who can separate the mirrors as much as possible to make the biggest maze, or use the most mirrors to make the mirror maze, or even shine the light around a corner and down a hallway. Come up with your own challenges, too! ◆

Fig. 2: Set up your mirror maze.

Creative Enrichment

Have you seen movies where the good guy or gal tries to get into a secret room protected by a laser security fence? If one of the laser beams is touched, an alarm will go off, and the villains will come running. You can make a laser maze, too! Use your mirrors and set up an entire maze down a dark hallway. Shine your laser off all the mirrors and onto a target at the end of the hall. Then, try to crawl under, hop, or step over the laser beams and make your way down the hall. Have someone watch where the laser beam ends up. If you accidentally touch the laser beam, you will block the light from reaching the target. If you make it all the way down the hall without causing the light on the target to go off, you win—but then, try to reverse your trip down the hall!

The Science Behind the Fun

When you turn the light on in a room, what happens? The room lights up, right? Yes, but there is a little more going on than meets the eye. In this lab, you turned on the flashlight. Light from the flashlight went outward and hit a series of mirrors. A little of the light that hit the mirrors traveled back to your eyes, which allowed you to see the mirrors. More of the light reflected off the mirrors, and then that light ended up shining on your object at the end of the mirror maze. How did you see the object, then? Light went outward from the flashlight, reflected off the mirrors, and then reflected off the object until some of that light traveled to your eyes and you saw the object. All this happens at a really fast speed, because light travels at 186,000 miles per second (300,000 km per second). Can you see a beam of light as it travels in the middle of a room? No! Light needs to hit something and then that light needs to shine into your eyes for you to see an object.

Stars, including our Sun, shine in the sky because they make their own light. Light from stars shines outward. Some of the light from the Sun hits our eyes, which allows us to see the Sun (don't look directly at the Sun!). Some of the Sun's light reflects off the planets and then to our eyes, which allows us to see the planets. That's one big difference between stars and planets. Stars make light, and planets reflect light.

Glowing Water

 Time

5 minutes

 Materials

- 2 clear drinking glasses
- Tonic water
- Tap water
- Your science notebook
- Pencil

 Safety Tips and Setup Hints

- This lab only works if you use tonic water that has quinine (pronounced KWY-nine) in it. Look for "contains quinine" or "tonic water with quinine" on the label. It is the quinine that causes the effect we will see.
- Do this lab on a sunny day, especially around the time when the Sun is highest in the sky.

A special kind of water can glow and show you what your eyes normally can't see.

Instructions

Step 1: Pour tonic water into one glass so it is mostly full. Pour tap water into the other glass so it is mostly full. Observe the tonic water and the tap water while you have them inside the house. See anything interesting? (Fig. 1)

Step 2: Take the full glasses and the black paper or plastic outside in the sunlight, and set up the glasses on a table or something sturdy. Make sure you know which glass has which water. (Fig. 2)

Step 3: Look at the surfaces of the tap water and tonic water as they sit out in the sunlight. What do you see now? (Fig. 3)

Step 4: Try this lab at different times of day. What do you notice when you do it around 8 or 9 a.m., around noon or 1 p.m., and around 3 or 4 p.m.? Try this lab at different times of year. What do you notice when you do it in the winter versus the summer? Write your observations in your notebook to compare. ✦

Fig. 1: Pour tonic water into one glass and tap water into the other glass.

Fig. 2: Set up your tonic and tap waters outside.

Creative Enrichment

You can detect UV light with more than just tonic water. Look for UV-sensitive (or "Sun sensitive") beads, flying discs, paper, wristbands, or clothing. These materials change colors when they are exposed to UV light. There are many experiments you can do with these materials. Take them out at different times of day to see how the color is affected. Take them out when it is sunny, partly cloudy, and completely cloudy to see if there is still enough UV light to make them change color. Try smearing different sunscreens on them and leave them out to see what happens. Test different sunglasses for UV protection. See if different clothes or materials might provide some UV protection. Take pictures during your experiments so you can compare the colors later. Use your imagination to come up with more ideas. The sky is the limit!

Fig. 3: See the water glowing?

The Science Behind the Fun

Our Sun gives off lots of different kinds of energy. The energy our eyes can detect is called "visible light." In Lab 28, "Can You See the Light" (see page 84), you used a camera to see a type of light our eyes can't see, called "infrared light." In this lab, we used tonic water to detect another type of light our eyes can't see, called "ultraviolet light." "Ultra" in "ultraviolet" means "beyond," so the word *ultraviolet* means "beyond the violet" or beyond the violet color of light in the rainbow.

You may have heard of ultraviolet, or UV, light. There are three groups of UV light, based on how much energy the UV light has. UVA light, which is the lowest-energy UV light, is given off by black lightbulbs. We can see a little of the visible light from black lights as a purple color, but much of the light from the bulb is UVA light our eyes can't see. Some paints react to UVA light by turning bright colors. Our skin reacts to UVA light from the Sun by tanning. UVB light has more energy than UVA light, and it is UVB light that gives us a sunburn. You can get a sunburn even when it is cloudy because UVB light can pass through clouds. You can also get nasty sunburns when you are on snow or at the beach because snow and sand reflect UVB light. There is a third type of UV light, called "UVC." It has even more energy than UVB light, but none of the UVC light reaches the ground because of a special layer in our atmosphere: the ozone layer.

The ozone layer is about 15 miles (25 km) above the Earth's surface. The ozone layer does not block UVA light, it blocks most UVB light, and it blocks all UVC light. Without an ozone layer, all the Sun's UV light would hit the ground, and this would be very, very bad for life on Earth.

"Measuring" the Speed of Light

 Time

5 minutes

 Materials

- Microwave oven
- 2 sturdy dinner-size paper plates
- Plain chocolate bar
- Ruler or tape measure
- Calculator that can display at least 11 digits at once

 Safety Tips and Setup Hints

- Do not use a regular plate for this lab. It will absorb energy and give you incorrect results.
- If your microwave oven contains a turntable to rotate food, remove the turntable plate. The turntable allows food to cook evenly, and you want the chocolate to cook unevenly for this lab to work best.
- Be careful when handling chocolate that has been melted in the microwave. It may be very hot and could cause burns if touched, and, if it is in the microwave for too long, it will begin to burn.

Calculating the speed of light is as easy as pie? No. It's as easy as melting chocolate!

Fig. 1: Two plates and a chocolate bar

Instructions

Step 1: Remove the glass turntable from your microwave. Place one paper plate upside down on the floor of the microwave. Place the second paper plate right side up on top of the first plate. The bottoms of both plates should touch each other. Place the chocolate bar on the top plate. If your bar has a flat side, place it flat side up. (Fig. 1)

Step 2: Microwave the chocolate bar at full power for twenty-five to fifty seconds, or until you start to see melted chocolate spots.

Step 3: Measure the distance between the "hot spots" of melted chocolate using your ruler. You can use inches or centimeters. Work quickly! The spot of melted chocolate may spread, making your measurement more difficult or less accurate. (Fig. 2)

Step 4: Multiply this measured distance by two. Then, multiply that calculated number by 2,450,000,000. This will be your calculation for the speed of light, often abbreviated as "c." If you measured the chocolate hot spot distance in inches, your "c" will be in inches per second; if you measured the hot spot distance in centimeters, your "c" will be in centimeters per second. (Fig. 3) ◆

Fig. 2: Measure the distance between the melted hot spots.

Creative Enrichment

Do you get easier-to-measure hot spots if you use chocolate chips? How about using regular-size chips versus miniature chips? White chocolate? Dark chocolate? A plate full of chocolate sprinkles, mini marshmallows, or whipped egg whites? What do these changes do to your calculated results?

Fig. 3: Calculate the speed of light.

The Science Behind the Fun

"Visible light," the type of light our eyes can see, travels at a constant speed, called the "speed of light." Microwaves are another form of light and also travel at this same speed. While our eyes cannot see microwave energy, we can see the "imprint" of these microwaves as melted chocolate hot spots.

Wavelength is how scientists tell different kinds of energy apart. Radio waves have the longest wavelengths, and gamma rays have extremely short wavelengths. The distance between the melted spots measures half a wavelength of the microwaves emitted by your oven. We first multiplied the **hot spot distance** by **2** to determine the span of a whole wavelength.

The speed of light is calculated as *wavelength multiplied by frequency*. The number 2,450,000,000 is the frequency of most modern microwaves: 2,450,000,000 waves that pass by a given point in a second. Therefore, **your wavelength in inches or centimeters** multiplied by **2,450,000,000 waves per second** gives you **the speed of light in inches or centimeters per second**.

The speed of light in air is 11,799,312,883 inches per second, or 29,970,254,724 centimeters per second. So, how close were you? Your result might be off by a bit, but this is absolutely to be expected. There is uncertainty in your hot spot measurement because the hot spots are extended areas, not single points—but if you got anywhere close to the right answer, you did a great job!

Drop, Drop, Drop!

Time

5 minutes

Materials

- 1 small ball, such as a tennis ball
- A few pieces of paper tightly crumpled into a ball the same size as the tennis ball
- Camera that can record video

Safety Tips and Setup Hints

- You will need two people to do this lab, one to drop the balls and one to record the drops using a camera. If you don't have a camera, that's okay! Just have both people take turns dropping the balls and carefully watching the drops.
- Use a ruler to check to make sure your two balls are the same size.
- The person recording the video should stand a few feet (about 1 m) away from the person dropping the balls. Make sure the camera can record the whole drop from start to finish without the person doing the recording having to move the camera at all.

Do heavier things drop faster than lighter things? There is only one way to find out. Try it!

Fig. 2: Drop, drop, drop!

Creative Enrichment

When NASA landed the Mars Exploration Rovers *Spirit* and *Opportunity* on Mars in January 2004, they needed to slow down the rovers as they were falling through Mars's air to the surface. How did they do this? Parachutes! Parachutes are designed to catch the air to slow something to a safe speed, just like a falling leaf or piece of paper catches air. Try to make the best parachute you can. Use materials such as paper, newspaper, string, fabric, or anything else you can find to make your parachutes. Look for parachute designs online or in books and use them to design your own. Attach a small object to your parachute, drop it, and time it to see how long it takes to fall. What worked best?

Fig. 1: Get ready to drop the two balls.

Instructions

Step 1: If you are using a stepladder, carefully go up the stepladder and have the second person hand you the two balls. If you are not using a stepladder, hold the two balls up over your head at the same height, one in each hand. If you are using a camera, get the camera ready to record the video. (Fig. 1)

Step 2: Record a video as both balls are dropped at exactly the same time from exactly the same height. (Fig. 2)

Step 3: Review the video to see when the balls hit the floor (if you can, play them in slow motion, too). Make sure you repeat the experiment several times. What do you notice? ◆

The Science Behind the Fun

Over two thousand years ago, a Greek scientist named Aristotle (pronounced AIR-us-tot-tul) said that if two objects were the same size and shape but one weighed more than the other, the heavier object should fall faster than the lighter object and hit the ground first. It seems this would make sense, right?

About four hundred years ago, Galileo did experiments to try out this idea. By rolling small balls down tracks and timing them, he showed that two objects dropped from the same height will hit the ground at about the same time. Isaac Newton later used what Galileo and others had worked on to develop his Law of Gravity.

When you did your experiment the first time, did you see the two balls hit the ground around the same time? Hopefully, it was pretty close, but there are several reasons why they might not have. Maybe you tried to hold the balls at the same height but one of your hands was a little higher than the other, or maybe you tried to drop them at the same time but one fell from your hand a little before the other. If you did this experiment outside, maybe a wind gust pushed the ball of paper a little. This is why it was important to do this lab several times so you could try to make your results as accurate as possible.

This experiment was also done on the Moon during the *Apollo 15* mission in 1971. Astronaut David Scott dropped a hammer and a falcon feather from a height of about 5 feet (1.6 m). There is no air on the Moon to slow the feather, so when Astronaut Scott dropped them, the two objects hit the Moon's surface at the same time. You can see a video of this experiment on NASA's Astronomy Picture of the Day website, posted on November 1, 2011: apod.nasa.gov/apod/ap111101.html.

LAB
34

Round and Round

 Time

5 minutes

 Materials

- Glow necklaces

 Safety Tips and Setup Hints

- Do this lab in a completely dark room, but make sure the floor is clear so you don't trip.

- The number of glow necklaces you need will depend on the number of people doing this lab. You should work in groups of three, with one glow necklace per group. Glow necklaces are available at party supply stores.

- If you do not have glow neck-laces, you will just need to "light up" one person without lighting the others in the group. One way is to turn on a small flashlight and put it in a paper bag. Have one person hold the paper bag. Or, wear a glow stick on a string like a necklace.

If you can't see something, how do you know it is there? Watch something you CAN see.

Instructions

Step 1: One person will represent a distant star. Have this person put a glow necklace around his or her neck. (Fig. 1)

Step 2: A second person should lock hands with the person wearing the necklace. A third person will pretend to be the astronomer observing the group from Earth. (Fig. 2)

Step 3: Turn off the lights in the room so it is dark. The pair should carefully twirl in a circle while holding hands. What does the observer from Earth see? (Fig. 3)

Fig. 1: Wear a glow necklace.

Creative Enrichment

Create a music piece or find a piece of music to go along with your black hole orbit twirls. What would your orbiting star *sound* like?

The Science Behind the Fun

In 1964 scientists saw something interesting in the sky in the direction of the stars in the constellation Cygnus the Swan. (Cygnus is pronounced like the word *big*: SIG-nuhs.) When they looked at that part of the sky using a special telescope, they saw that something was giving off X-rays, a type of light our eyes can't see. What was it? When they looked at the same spot using telescopes that could see "visible" light, which is the light our eyes can see, they didn't see anything. Nearby, though, was a star. The star itself was a normal star, but it was doing something interesting. About every five days, the star seemed to be orbiting, or going around, the area that was giving off those X-rays. They gave this strange spot a name: Cygnus X-1. What was this strange thing?

What they figured out was that the light they *could* see was telling them about something the*y could not* see. The object they couldn't see using their visible light telescopes was a "black hole." Black holes are strange. Imagine a huge star, even bigger than our Sun, and the star has reached its end. Imagine that gravity pulls almost everything in the star into a ball the size of a large city, and nothing, not even light, can escape it. That's REALLY hard to imagine, isn't it? Well, this is a black hole.

Fig. 2: Get ready to spin!

Fig. 3: Round and round!

In this lab, the person with the glow necklace or flashlight played the part of the star that astronomers can see. The other person played the part of the object that we can't see. As the two twirled around each other, the observer from Earth could spot the moving star but not the other object.

Free Fall

Materials

- 1 paper or foam cup
- Something to poke a hole in the cup, such as a sharpened pencil
- 1 bucket filled with water

Safety Tips and Setup Hints

- Do this lab outside or in the bathtub. It will be a little messy.
- Be careful poking holes in the cup. You don't want to poke holes in your hand!
- If it is easier to see this lab by filming it, have a second person film you as you drop the cup of water.

You don't have to go to space to see free fall. Let gravity do the work for you!

Fig. 1: Poke two holes in the cup.

Fig. 2: Watch water falling from the cup.

Instructions

Step 1: Carefully poke two holes near the bottom of the empty cup along the sides of the cup. (Fig. 1)

Step 2: Cover the holes with your fingers and fill the cup with water. Don't let the water out of the holes. Hold the cup over the bucket and uncover the holes. What happens to the water? (Fig. 2)

Step 3: Cover the holes with your fingers again, and fill the cup with water. This time, hold the cup high. Make a prediction for what you think will happen to the water and the cup when you drop it. Then, uncover the holes to start to let water out, and then drop the cup as the water is falling out of the holes. What happened to the water this time? (Fig. 3) ✦

Fig. 3: Drop the cup as the water is falling.

Creative Enrichment

On several different space flights, NASA astronauts took everyday toys into space to test whether they worked the same way in space as they worked on Earth. To see one of these videos, do a search online for "NASA International Toys in Space." Before NASA shows you what happens to those toys, make some predictions for how you think they will work in space. Watch the videos. Were you right?

Did you know all the weightless scenes of the movie *Apollo 13* were filmed in NASA's KC-135 airplane? The actors look like they were weightless—because they actually were! The movie's director used NASA's airplane for six months. The next time you watch the movie, look for all these free fall scenes. Amazing!

The Science Behind the Fun

Was there anything surprising about this lab? When you held the cup full of water and uncovered the holes, your hand kept the cup from falling, but gravity allowed the water to flow through the holes to the ground. Then, you dropped the full cup of water when the holes were uncovered. Did you notice the water stopped falling out of the holes while the cup fell?

When the cup of water fell, the cup and the water fell at the same speed, just like when you dropped the two different balls in Lab 33, "Drop, Drop, Drop!" (see page 94). If water was supposed to keep falling out of the holes when you dropped the cup, it would mean the water would have to fall *faster* than the cup. As we found out, this isn't possible. The cup and the water fell at the same time at the same speed. For a split second, the cup and water were in free fall. If you were inside the cup when it dropped, you wouldn't feel gravity pulling down.

There is no way to make a "zero-gravity room" on Earth, so when NASA wants to train astronauts for flying in space, one way they do it is to create free fall in an airplane. The plane is called a "KC-135," but the best name for it is the *Vomit Comet*. The pilot steers the plane into a steep climb, just like you are going up a steep climb on a roller coaster. While the plane is climbing, passengers are pushed into their seats and feel like they weigh more than they do on the ground. As the plane levels out and starts to dive, like going over the top of a roller coaster, passengers get about thirty seconds of weightlessness, sometimes called "free fall." Then, the pilot starts to pull the plane out of its dive. Why the name *Vomit Comet*? Well, the pilot does this process over and over, as many as thirty or forty times in a row! Do you think you would have fun on the *Vomit Comet*?

Exploring Our Solar System

Many people ask, "Who discovered the planets?" Well, people have always known about Mercury, Venus, Mars, Jupiter, and Saturn. They kind of look like stars, but they don't move in the sky exactly like the stars do, and ancient people noticed this. Greek people from long ago called these objects "planetes." The word *planetes* meant "wanderers." The planetes appeared to wander around the sky. What does the word *planetes* remind you of? Of course—planets! That is where the English word *planet* comes from.

Now, ancient people did not know what planets were. We started to know a lot more about them when we could look at them with telescopes. When Galileo and others looked at them with their telescopes, they could see that they weren't points of light. Telescopes showed they were round, and as our telescopes got better and better, they could see light and dark areas on Mars, stripes on Jupiter, and a ring around Saturn. People used telescopes to find Uranus, Neptune, Pluto, asteroids, and lots of comets. Then, instead of just counting things and seeing how they move, we wanted to know what they were like and how things work there.

In this next set of activities, you'll learn why some things in our Solar System look the way they do, compare some places to others, find out why Mars really isn't red, why you probably wouldn't vacation on Venus, and you'll see our Sun's spotty face. You'll get to know our Solar System in fun ways!

As Saturn goes around the Sun, its tilt lets us see different parts at different times. This tilt also makes seasons on Saturn.
Credit: NASA and The Hubble Heritage Team (STScI/AURA)

LAB 36

Sorting Our Solar System

Materials

- At least 30 pictures of objects or places in our Solar System (the more pictures, the better!)
- Several pieces of paper
- Pencil, pen, or marker

Safety Tips and Setup Hints

- NASA has lots of pictures of objects in our Solar System. Use a mix of close-up and faraway images. You can see and print them from:
  - **Planets and dwarf planets:** photojournal.jpl.nasa.gov
  - **Solar System objects:** hubblesite.org/gallery/album/ solar_system
  - **Comets and asteroids:** photojournal.jpl.nasa.gov/ target/Other
- You can also cut out pictures of planets, moons, asteroids, and comets from astronomy and science magazines. See if your local library is having a used book or magazine sale, or contact a local astronomy club to ask if they have copies of astronomy magazines a member wants to give away.

Scientists put things in groups all the time. Try your hand at sorting our Solar System.

Instructions

Step 1: Lay out the pictures so you can see them all. (Fig. 1)

Step 2: One person will sort the pictures into two or more groups of his or her own choice. Be creative! You do not have to choose groups like "planets," "moons," "asteroids," or "comets." Choose groups based on colors, shapes, whether the objects contain craters (or not), objects that are close to the Sun, objects that are far from the Sun, rocky things, icy things, things with stripes, round things versus things that aren't round, or anything else you would like to choose. There are no right answers, and you do not have to use all the pictures. Make labels for each group, but do not show the labels to the other person yet. (Fig. 2)

Step 3: A second person will try to figure out the groups chosen by the first person. Did you figure out the groups correctly?

Step 4: Switch roles. The second person should now try to make new groups, and the first person should try to figure out what they are. Do this as many times as you want!

Fig. 1: Display your pictures.

Creative Enrichment

When you are done with this lab, make an art collage of as many pretty Solar System pictures as you can find. Use real pictures for some of your images. Try making sketches of some images using interesting colors. Use other materials to add to some of the pictures, such as glitter, construction paper, tissue paper, ribbon, or natural things, such as leaves, dried flowers, twigs, or grasses. Group your pictures any way you want!

The Science Behind the Fun

Did you notice when you did this lab you could put the same picture into different groups? Scientists like to group things, too. In our Solar System, we have one star: our Sun. There are eight planets: Mercury, Venus, Earth, Mars, Jupiter, Saturn, Uranus, and Neptune, and we know of at least 173 moons. We can make many groups of planets, such as "planets with rings" and "planets with no rings," or "large planets" and "small planets," or "planets with moons" and "planets without moons." There are many thousands of comets, which are city-size chunks of ice and rock. There are more than two hundred thousand asteroids that are a few tens of feet (a few meters) across to the largest asteroid, which is 590 miles (950 km) across. Even asteroids can be grouped, such as "asteroids that pass close to Earth," "asteroids between Mars and Jupiter," and others.

There are at least five dwarf planets in our Solar System, which means that these objects are round and they orbit the Sun. One of the dwarf planets is Ceres (pronounced SEER-reez), which is also an asteroid. But wait—how can something be an asteroid AND a dwarf planet? How can something be in more than one group? You probably put the same picture in more than one group, and this happens in science all the time. Both groups are correct!

Fig. 2: Sort your pictures into groups.

LAB 37

Will I Hear a Sound in Space?

Time
15 minutes

Materials
- Small wooden craft stick
- Small bell
- Masking tape
- Sticky adhesive putty
- Glass bottle with a screw-top lid
- Matches

Safety Tips and Setup Hints
- If you need a bell, use one from a pet toy or a holiday decoration.
- **Don't use a plastic bottle for this lab!** Flames and plastic create very dangerous gases, and the plastic might melt. A glass bottle that holds a liquid to drink would work well. Just wash the bottle and make sure it is completely dry.
- An adult should handle the matches. When the matches go out inside the bottle, be careful. The bottle may be hot where the matches were touching it.
- Adhesive putty or sticky putty looks a little like soft clay, but it is used to stick paper or other lightweight things to walls without using tape. It's available at office supply stores.

Can you hear noise in space? Try this experiment to see if you are right!

Fig. 1: Tape the bell to the stick.

Fig. 3: Put the lid on the bottle.

Fig. 2: Attach the stick to the lid.

Instructions

Step 1: Tape the bell to one end of the craft stick. Shake it to make sure the bell still rings. (Fig. 1)

Step 2: Use a blob of sticky putty to attach the other end of the stick to the inside of the lid of the glass bottle. When you let go of the stick, it should stay attached to the lid. (Fig. 2)

Step 3: Put the craft stick into the bottle and screw on the lid. The stick shouldn't touch the sides of the bottle. Shake the bottle a little to make sure you can hear the bell and the stick stays attached to the inside of the lid. If the stick comes loose, add more sticky putty. (Fig. 3)

Fig. 4: An adult adds two lit matches to the bottle.

Step 4: Take the lid off the bottle. Have an adult light two matches and drop them into the bottle. Screw the lid back on the bottle. Make sure the matches don't touch the stick or the bell! (Fig. 4)

Step 5: Wait a few seconds for the flames to go out. Then, shake the bottle again. Now what do you hear? ◆

Creative Enrichment

Want to make your own sticky putty for this lab? There are two ways to do it. First, grab an old glue stick that is too dry to glue things together. If you only have a new glue stick, leave it out with the cap off for a few days to dry it. Scoop out the glue and squish it around in your fingers and hands. If it's still too soft, add a little baby powder. It should be like putty. The second way is to mix two parts liquid white school glue and one part liquid clothes starch. Stir with a spoon, and adjust the amounts to get a putty. (Before you use your sticky putty on walls or other surfaces, test it to make sure it won't leave a mark or peel paint off the walls.)

The Science Behind the Fun

How does sound work? Sound is a type of energy. Think of something that makes a sound, such as a guitar string. When a guitar string vibrates, or moves quickly from side to side, the string pushes against air particles next to it. These vibrating particles bump into particles close to them and cause those particles to vibrate. These vibrations keep going, and if there is still enough energy from those bumping air particles that they bump into air particles next to your eardrum, then that vibrating air causes your eardrum to vibrate. This works for more than just air, too. Have you ever gone swimming and heard sounds under water? Vibrating water particles can also cause your eardrum to vibrate.

We often say, "space is empty," but that's not quite right. There are very, very few particles in space, so there are very, very few particles to vibrate. There are far too few particles to vibrate human eardrums, so you would *not* hear sounds in space. In this lab, you used matches inside the bottle, and the match flames used up some of the oxygen in the bottle, and then the flames went out. There was less air inside the bottle than outside, so there were fewer particles for the bell to vibrate. The sound was lower than when you rung the bell the first time!

So, if people can't hear sounds in space, how do we talk to astronauts in space? We use radio waves. While radio waves are a type of light our eyes can't see, we can use special equipment to detect those radio waves and turn them into vibrations, which vibrate air particles, which vibrate your eardrum, which you hear as sound!

How to "See" a Surface When You Can't See a Surface

Time
1 hour

Materials

- Plastic straw
- Ruler or tape measure with centimeter marks
- Permanent marker
- 1 cardboard box with a separate lid, such as a shoe box
- Pencil
- Scissors (or something sharp to poke holes in the box lid)
- A set of plastic snap-together bricks
- Your science notebook

Safety Tips and Setup Hints

- An adult should be the one to make the holes in the box lid.

There are some places in the Solar System we can't see easily. So, how do we see them?

Instructions

Step 1: Lay the straw on a table and put the zero end of your ruler at one end of the straw. Using the permanent marker, put a small mark on the straw every centimeter along its whole length. Don't let the straw roll! Label each centimeter (1, 2, 3, and so on) along the straw. (Fig. 1)

Step 2: Lay your box lid on the table and put the zero end of your ruler at one of the short edges of the lid. Using the pencil, put a small mark along the long edge of the lid every two centimeters. Do the same thing along the other long edge (and make sure your marks line up).

Then, put the zero end of your ruler at one of the long edges of the lid. Using the pencil, put a small mark along the short edge of the lid every two centimeters. Do the same thing along the other short edge.

Finally, line up the marks with the ruler along opposite edges and draw a line with the pencil to connect the dots in a straight line. Do this for all the marks along the long edges of the box and along the short edges of the box. You should end up with a set of squares all over the top of the box. (Why use pencil? If your marks aren't in the right place, you can erase them and remeasure.) (Fig. 2)

Step 3: Where your grid lines come together, have an adult make a hole using scissors or the pointy end of a sharp knife. You should end up with a grid of holes all over the top of your box. Make sure the holes are big enough for your straw to go through easily. (Fig. 3)

Fig. 1: Turn your straw into a ruler.

Fig. 2: Draw a grid on your box lid.

Fig. 3: Poke holes in the top of the box.

The Science Behind the Fun

There are places in our Solar System where we can't easily see what's there. How do we "see" these surfaces, then? The answer is RADAR. "RADAR" stands for "RAdio Detection and Ranging." A radar system uses radio waves pointed toward a surface. The radio waves travel at the speed of light, hit the surface, and travel back to the system. Radar systems can tell us things, such as how high a surface is, what temperature it is, or what the surface looks like. NASA's *Cassini* spacecraft used radar to study the hazy surface of Saturn's moon Titan, and NASA's *Magellan* spacecraft used radar to study the cloud-covered surface of Venus. In our lab, we couldn't send out radio or sound waves, so we used the straw as our way to figure out where the top of the surface was inside the box. You can change the surface inside the box as often as you like! Challenge your friends or family to the same lab. How did they do?

Step 4: Have someone else make a "planet surface" inside the box so you don't see it. Have that person snap different bricks together and make a surface with different heights all over the inside of the box. Don't peek! Your partner should put the lid on the box without showing the inside to you. (Fig. 4)

Step 5: In your science notebook, draw a grid that matches your lid. If your lid is six holes wide and fifteen holes long, draw the same grid in your science notebook. Starting at one end of the box, put the zero end of the straw through the first hole in the box. Push the straw in until it hits something and stops. Look at your straw and record the measurement in your notebook. If the straw ends up between marks, record the number of the first mark you can see above the hole. Do the same for all the holes, and record measurements for every hole in your notebook. (Fig. 5)

Step 6: Look at your notebook. Can you tell which parts of the surface in the box are taller and which parts are shorter? Lift the lid to see if you are right! ◆

Creative Enrichment

Look at your measurements of the surface inside the box. How would you show higher parts of the surface on a flat piece of paper? How would you show lower parts? Try to draw a map just by using your grid and those measurements.

Fig. 4: Make a bumpy planet surface inside the box.

Fig. 5: Measure the inside of the box using the straw.

LAB 39

Hole-y Surfaces!

Let's see how craters are made and how we can learn about surfaces by studying them.

Time

15 to 20 minutes

Materials

- 1 pan about 8 to 12 inches (20 to 30 cm) long and about 4 inches (10 cm) deep
- Newspaper or plastic sheeting
- Enough flour to fill your pan about three-fourths full (the amount will depend on the size of your pan)
- 1 or 2 small bottles of colored sugar
- About ½ to 1 cup (43 to 86 g) of cocoa powder
- Flour sifter or small fine-mesh strainer
- A handful of small rocks or marbles of various sizes (no more than 2 inches [5 cm] in diameter)
- Ruler or tape measure

Safety Tips and Setup Hints

- Do not substitute hot chocolate mix for the cocoa powder. There is not enough color contrast between the mix and the flour to make the cratering effects stand out.
- For easy cleanup, do this lab outside or put newspaper or plastic sheeting under your pan.

Instructions

Step 1: Fill your pan about halfway full of flour. Then, shake a layer of colored sugar over the surface of the flour, covering the flour completely with the colored sugar. (Fig. 1)

Step 2: With the sifter, sift a layer of flour over the sugared layer, filling your pan about three-fourths of the way total. Next, sift a layer of cocoa powder over the flour, covering the flour completely. You should end up with a pan with several layers; from the bottom up, your pan will contain flour, then colored sugar above, then flour, and finally cocoa powder on the top. (Fig. 2)

Step 3: Drop a rock into the flour. You can see the different layers represented by the different colors of materials. What happened? Which material went farthest? Which material didn't travel quite as far? (Fig. 3)

Step 4: Try dropping rocks of different sizes from the same height, measuring the height using your ruler or tape measure. What differences do you see in the craters? Next, drop rocks of the same size from different heights, representing objects traveling at different speeds. How are your craters the same or different? (If your pan is small, you may have to reapply the flour, sugar, and cocoa powder layers periodically.)

Fig. 1: Sprinkle colored sugar on your flour.   Fig. 2: You are ready to create some craters!

The Science Behind the Fun

A crater can form when an object from space smashes into the surface of a world. The hole is usually roughly circular in shape. The size of the resulting crater depends on many different factors, such as the speed, density, size, or angle of the impacting object, and the density of the surface that is struck. (Fig. 4)

Scientists are very interested in studying craters because they not only can tell you about the impact event itself, but this natural process has also excavated a way for you to see into a surface without having to dig the hole yourself! There are about 175 known impact craters on Earth and untold millions on many other worlds. Why don't we see many craters on Earth? Earth's surface is very geologically active, and the rocky surface is continually changing due to plate tectonics, volcanoes, and the weathering action of wind and water. Friction with Earth's atmosphere causes many smaller objects to burn up before reaching the surface, so only larger objects strike and create craters. In addition, 70 percent of Earth's surface is covered by water, meaning quite a few objects that are able to survive to the surface fall harmlessly into the ocean.

Creative Enrichment

You can try different types of materials in your cratering pan, representing different surfaces found in our Solar System:

Earth: Use the same flour/sugar/flour/cocoa powder surface, but after you make a few craters, use a mister or hand sprayer bottle to spray your craters lightly with water, representing weathering over time. What happens to your craters after five sprays as water interacts with them? Ten sprays? More sprays?

Wet Mars: Mix dirt and water to make mud, though don't make it soupy. This represents some of the Martian surfaces we have seen that seem to indicate that craters occurred on Mars when liquid water was just under the surface a long time ago. Make your craters using this surface. How do these craters differ from the others?

Frozen Mars: Freeze a thin layer of water in your pan for an hour or two, and then cover it with a layer of fine sand. This represents ice just below the Martian surface, something we have seen on Mars recently. You may have to throw your impactor vigorously to go through the ice layer. How are these frozen Mars craters different from the wet Mars craters?

Credit: NASA/JPL/ University of Arizona

Fig. 4: This is a 100-foot-diameter (30 m) crater on the surface of Mars, the result of an impact that occurred sometime between July 2010 and May 2012. Material was thrown as far as nine miles (15 km) away.

Fig. 3: A very hole-y surface!

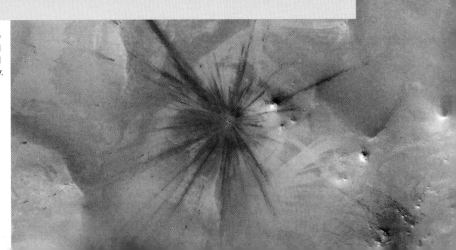

Would You Vacation on Venus?

 Time

2 to 3 hours

 Materials

- 2 glass Mason jars with lids or large glass juice bottles with lids
- 2 thermometers small enough to fit inside the jars with the lids on
- 1 container of play dough or play clay
- 1 tablespoon (14 g) baking soda
- 2 tablespoons (30 ml) vinegar

 Safety Tips and Setup Hints

- Do this lab during a sunny day around the time when the Sun is highest in the sky.
- Be very careful opening the jar with the baking soda and vinegar, as it might splash out at your face. When you open the jar, point it away from your face, put a towel over the lid, and open the jar very, very slowly. Have an adult nearby just in case!
- If you have safety glasses or goggles, wear them when handling the jar with the baking soda and vinegar.

Venus is the second planet from the Sun, but it is the hottest planet. Why?

Instructions

Step 1: Put one of the thermometers into a glass jar and twist the lid closed. Make sure you can read the thermometer. Seal the lid by covering it completely with a layer of play clay. (Fig. 1)

Step 2: Pour the baking soda into the other jar and put in the thermometer. As quickly as possible, pour in the vinegar and twist the lid closed so everything is trapped in the jar. Seal the lid by covering it completely with a layer of play clay. (Fig. 2)

Step 3: Take both jars outside and put them in a sunny spot. Every ten minutes, go out and record the temperature in both jars, for a total of two to three hours. What do you notice? (Fig. 3)

Fig. 1: Seal a thermometer in one jar.

The Science Behind the Fun

Have you ever been inside a greenhouse? If you have, you might have noticed the air is warmer inside the greenhouse than outside. Sunlight enters the greenhouse through the glass or plastic windows, and the light hits the floor. The floor gives off heat, and the heat is trapped by the windows, warming up the air inside. Greenhouses are able to keep the air inside a comfortable temperature, even when the outside air temperature might be close to freezing.

On Earth, the same thing happens. Light from the Sun hits the ground, and the ground gives off heat. In Earth's air, there are many gases that trap heat, such as carbon dioxide and methane. Without greenhouse gases, Earth would be a lot colder. The right amounts of greenhouse gases make Earth livable.

Venus is completely covered by clouds. Light from the Sun filters through the clouds, hits the ground, and the ground gives off heat. Venus has much, much more air than Earth does, and almost all the air is carbon dioxide. This traps a lot more heat, making Venus roast at 867°F (464°C). The air moves around, even heating the side facing away from the Sun to the same temperature. In this lab, we created a "mini Venus" in the jar by adding vinegar and baking soda, which created carbon dioxide gas and water. The additional carbon dioxide in the jar was enough to trap a little more heat and raise the temperature in that jar compared to the other one.

On Mercury, the side facing the Sun reaches about 800°F (427°C), but it basically has no air and no way to move the heat from the warm side to the cold side. Even though Mercury is closer to the Sun than Venus, Venus is much better at holding on to the heat and moving warm air around, so it gets hotter.

Fig. 2: Seal a thermometer in the other jar with vinegar and baking soda.

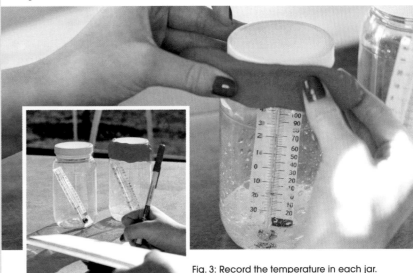

Fig. 3: Record the temperature in each jar.

Creative Enrichment

You can use jars, two-liter bottles, and gallon-size (3.75 L) plastic bottles to make mini greenhouses. There are lots of webpages and videos online to help you. Search for words, such as *garden in a jar* or *plastic bottle terrarium*. This is a great idea for growing plants in the late fall, winter, and early spring when it might be too cold outside to grow anything. Try growing herbs, such as basil or parsley, or plants, such as lettuce or spinach. If you have pets, check to make sure the plants you grow are safe for pets in case they like to munch on your garden, too.

Is the Red Planet Actually Red?

Time
3 to 7 days

Materials
- 1 or 2 steel wool pads
- Sharp scissors
- 2 small containers of sand or small pebbles
- Spray bottle filled with water
- Plastic wrap

Safety Tips and Setup Hints
- Have an adult cut up the steel wool into small pieces using sharp scissors. Be careful. The steel wool pieces can be sharp. Use heavy work gloves when handling them, and do not rub your eyes or skin after handling the steel wool. Wash your hands when you are done.

We call Mars the "Red Planet." Is it?

Instructions

Step 1: Carefully mix the steel wool pieces with the sand or pebbles in one container. Do not do anything to the sand in the other container. (Fig. 1)

Step 2: Spray the top of the sand or pebbles in both containers lightly with the water five to seven times. (Fig. 2)

Step 3: Cover the containers with plastic wrap. (Fig. 3)

Step 4: Every day, spray the sand in both containers again and cover the containers again. After a few days, compare the sand or pebbles in both containers. Are there any differences? (Fig. 4)

This feature on Mars is called Ma'adim Valles. *Ma'adim* is the Hebrew word for the planet Mars. Ma'adim Valles is likely a dried river that flowed north to the crater at the top of the picture, called Gusev (GOO-sev) Crater. Gusev Crater is where NASA's *Spirit* rover landed in January 2004. This picture of Ma'adim Valles was taken by one of NASA's *Viking* orbiters in the 1970s.

Credit: NASA/JPL–Caltech

The Science Behind the Fun

When you think of the color red, what do you think of? Maybe you think of stop signs, apples, or exit signs. Have you seen pictures of Mars? Is Mars the same red color as those other red things? Not exactly. Mars may be called the Red Planet, but it really isn't bright red at all. Parts of Mars can be reddish brown and other parts are gray. These reddish and gray minerals on Mars are really just the same mineral, called "hematite" (pronounced HE-muh-tite). The red version of this mineral is the same as the gray version; the red version is just the gray version ground up into a smaller powder, causing it to look red. The rust you made in your bowl is a cousin to the hematite we have found on Mars.

Was Mars wet in the distant past? Yes it was! Scientists have seen many signs of long ago liquid water on Mars, including evidence of gullies, streams, hot springs, and dried riverbeds.

Creative Enrichment

Would you like to see places on Earth similar to Mars? Do a search online for pictures of these locations:

- Ubehebe Crater and Mars Hill, both in Death Valley National Park, California
- Mono Lake, California
- Channeled Scablands in Washington
- Volcanoes in Hawai'i Volcanoes National Park

Make a travel brochure for one of these spots. Find out where it is, how to get there, how to explore there safely, and how your chosen spot is like Mars. For even more fun, use your travel brochure to plan and lead a family trip! It's like going to Mars—only easier!

Fig. 1: Mix in the steel wool.

Fig. 2: Spray both containers with water.

Fig. 3: Cover both containers.

Fig. 4: What does the sand look like after a few days?

Looking for Life on Mars

Time

A few hours to a few days

Materials

- 3 glass Mason jars with lids
- 9 cups (3.15 L) of sand or tiny pebbles
- 4 teaspoons (24 g) of salt
- 4 teaspoons (18 g) of baking powder
- 2 packets of dry yeast (1 packet of yeast is about 2 teaspoons, or 9 g)
- 1 large pitcher
- 1 cup (200 g) of sugar
- 3 cups (710 ml) of warm water (100° to 110°F, or 37° to 43°C)
- Cookie sheet
- Your science notebook
- Pencil

Safety Tips and Setup Hints

- You will do this experiment twice. Pay attention to the amounts in the instructions.
- Label each jar so you can tell them apart later. The first jar should be labeled "salt," the second jar should be labeled "baking powder," and the third jar should be labeled "yeast."

The *Viking* spacecraft looked for signs of life on Mars in the 1970s. What did they find?

Instructions

Step 1: Fill each jar with 1½ cups (350 g) of sand. Pour 2 teaspoons of salt into the first jar. Pour 2 teaspoons of baking powder into the second jar. Pour one packet of yeast into the third jar. Put the lids on each jar.

Step 2: *Gently* shake the jars to mix the ingredients into the sand. Remove the lids. (Fig. 1)

Step 3: Pour ½ cup (100 g) of sugar into 1½ cups (about 300 ml) of warm water. Stir the water with a spoon until the sugar is dissolved. You'll know it is dissolved when you don't feel the crunchy sugar crystals when you stir the water, and the water will look clear again.

Step 4: Pour about ½ cup (about 120 ml) of sugar water into each jar. Put the jars onto the cookie sheet to prevent spills. (Fig. 2)

Step 5: Observe what happens in each jar, checking back every hour or so. Record the results in your science notebook. Let the jars sit overnight, and observe them the next day. What did you notice?

Step 6: Pour all the sand out of each jar (ask an adult where to put the sand). Clean each jar. Repeat the experiment by putting sand into each jar, and adding the salt, baking powder, and yeast into the jars. Use the same amounts as described in step 1. Put the lids on the jars, and gently shake the jars. Take the lids off the jars. This time, put all three jars into the freezer, and let them sit overnight or, even better, for a few days. Take the jars out of the freezer, and repeat the experiment by adding the warm sugar water to each jar. Observe what happens. What do you notice this time? ◆

Creative Enrichment

You can use yeast in other ways—such as making bread! There is a type of bread called "Amish Friendship Bread" that starts with flour, milk, sugar, and yeast. The sugar feeds the yeast, and the yeast gives off gas. Every few days more milk and flour are added, and sugar is added so the yeast has even more food to eat. After a few more days, the batter is ready to use, and some of it can be given away to friends so they can make their own friendship bread. Give it a try!

Fig. 1: Prepare your jars.

The Science Behind the Fun

In 1976 NASA landed two spacecraft on Mars, called *Viking 1* and *Viking 2*. One of the questions scientists hoped to answer was whether there was life on the surface of Mars. This would not be life like people or animals, but smaller life, such as bacteria. When chemicals are added to soil containing bacteria that can eat the chemicals as food, then the sample would give off gas as long as there is food to feed the bacteria. If there were no bacteria, then only a little gas or no gas at all would be released. What did NASA find out? There were mixed results. One experiment showed a release of gas, like you would see if life was there, but two other experiments didn't show any signs of life. Experiments on future Mars landers may help answer the question of whether there was, or is, life on Mars.

In this experiment, the sand represents Mars soil. The salt and baking powder represent different chemicals in Mars soil. The yeast represents bacteria. When the warm sugar water was added to the first set of sand in the jars, the yeast ate the sugar and gave off lots of gas for a while, until they ate all the sugar. In the second experiment, the jars were put into the freezer to represent the cold surface of Mars.

Fig. 2: Pour in the sugar water.

YEAST

Cool Crystals

Time

A few hours to overnight

Materials

- For Epsom salt crystals:
  - Small, deep bowl
  - ½ cup (120 ml) hot water from the faucet
  - ½ cup (120 g) Epsom salt
  - Food coloring (any color)
- For table salt crystals:
  - Small pot
  - 1 cup (240 ml) distilled water
  - Noniodized salt (amount will vary)
  - Piece of cardboard small enough to fit into the pot
  - Plate
- For the borax crystals:
  - Up to 4 cups (950 ml) of water
  - 1 Mason jar
  - Up to 1 cup (240 ml) of borax
  - Food coloring (any color)
  - Pipe cleaner (also called a "chenille stem")
  - 3 inches (7.5 cm) of string
  - Straw or pencil

(Continues on page 118)

You can make several kinds of crystals using everyday things.

Instructions

Step 1: For the Epsom salt crystals, pour the hot water into the bowl, add a few drops of food coloring, and stir in the Epsom salt until most of it dissolves. Some crunchy bits will still be at the bottom of the bowl. Put the bowl in the refrigerator. After a few days, check the bowl. What do you see? (Fig. 1)

Step 2: For the table salt crystals, boil the water in a small pot on the stove. Slowly stir salt into the boiling water until no more salt will dissolve. You will know enough is added when salt pieces stay on the bottom of the pot and the bottom of the pot will feel a little crunchy. Turn off the stove. (Fig. 2)

Step 3: Have an adult carefully soak a small piece of cardboard in the hot salty water. When it is soggy, put it on a plate, and put it in a warm spot in the sunlight outside. Watch it for a few hours as it dries out. What do you see? (Fig. 3)

Step 4: For the borax crystals, boil the water and carefully pour it into the jar. Stir in the borax until no more can dissolve. A few crunchy bits will be on the bottom of the jar. Put a few drops of food coloring into the jar. (Fig. 4)

(Continues on page 118)

Fig. 1: Make Epsom salt crystals.

Safety Tips and Setup Hints

(Continued from page 116)

- Make sure an adult helps with making these crystals, especially the parts using hot or boiling water. Be careful!

- Do not eat the Epsom salt crystals or the borax crystals. **They are not edible.** The salt crystals contain a lot of salt, so it is best not to eat them.

- For the table salt crystals, use salt that does not have iodine in it. It will be called "noniodized" salt.

- Epsom salt is available in the first-aid section of a drugstore and many grocery stores. Powdered borax is available in the laundry detergent section of a grocery store.

Step 5: Twist one end of the pipe cleaner into whatever shape you want. The shape should be able to fit into the jar. Tie a piece of string to the pipe cleaner handle. Tie the other end of the string to the straw or pencil so the pipe cleaner can hang into the jar without touching the bottom of the jar. Put the pipe cleaner into the borax water in the jar. Let the jar sit for a few days. Don't move it or touch it. What do you see?

Fig. 2: Make table salt crystals.

The Science Behind the Fun

If you live in a place where there is snow, catch a few snowflakes and look at them up close. Snowflakes are crystals, too! A crystal is a hard material made of bits that come together in patterns to form interesting shapes. Salt crystals usually form cube shapes, Epsom salt crystals form needle shapes, and other materials form different shapes.

Minerals also come in crystal shapes. These mineral crystals can tell us a lot. Some of the oldest known bits of Earth's crust are crystals called "zircon." Some types of meteorites contain different kinds of crystals, and we can learn about what the early Solar System was like from meteorites. Rovers on Mars have found crystals of gypsum (pronounced JIP-sum), which tells us that some parts of Mars had hot water springs. When the hot water dried, the gypsum crystals were left behind in the rock. We can learn about lots of surfaces in our Solar System by studying minerals and crystals!

Creative Enrichment

There are lots of recipes for making sugar crystals, also called "rock sugar candy." Look up a recipe online or in a kitchen science experiment book, and have an adult help you make it. Also, if you need something else to do with your box of borax after you make borax crystals, check out recipes online for making different types of slime. You can't eat the slime, but it is fun to make it!

Fig. 4: Make the borax water.

Fig. 3: Soak the cardboard in the salt water.

LAB 44

Spot Sunspots

Time

10 minutes each day

Materials

- Your science notebook
- 1 piece of white copy paper
- Pencil
- Marker
- Pinhole projector from Lab 14, "Make a Pinhole Projector" (see page 44)

Safety Tips and Setup Hints

- You'll need a fairly sunny day each time you do this lab.
- Do this lab around the time when the Sun is highest in the sky. Always go out at about the same time each day you do this.
- **Never look directly at the Sun**, and do not look through your pinhole or through your pinhole projector at the Sun! Doing so may *very quickly* cause eye damage or blindness.
- You may need someone else with you to hold your pinhole projector in place while you observe the image of the Sun.

You can see some of the largest spots on our Sun. Give it a try!

Instructions

Step 1: Set up your science notebook pages for your observations. Look back at your observations of the Sun for Lab 16, "How Can the Moon Cover the Sun?" (see page 50). There, you measured the size of the image of the Sun made by your pinhole projector. Put the piece of copy paper over your Sun drawing from that lab and trace the outer edge of the Sun in one corner of the page. Do this several times on the same piece of paper so you have lots of circles in rows and columns. Trace each circle carefully with a marker. Use a copy machine to make copies of this same page and put them in your science notebook so you can use the same page to make many observations (you'll also need one or two copies for Lab 45, "Our Spinning Sun" (page 122). (Fig. 1)

Step 2: On a sunny day, point the pinhole end of the projector at the Sun and look for an image of the Sun on your white screen inside the box. (Fig. 2)

Step 3: Move the box just a little. If you can see small dark spots on the image of the Sun that move along with the Sun's image when you move the box, stop and sketch the spots you see. If you notice any spots that don't move with the Sun's image, it means those spots are part of your piece of paper. You can ignore those. (Fig. 3)

Step 4: Over the course of days, weeks, or many months, repeat these observations and sketches as often as you can. Keep notes in your notebook, especially the dates of your observations. Look back at your observations after a while. What do you notice? ✦

Creative Enrichment

Make a batch of your favorite cupcakes or cookies and decorate each one to match current images of the Sun using various colors of icing, frosting, or candies. You can find the most current solar images on NASA's Solar Dynamics Observatory website: sdo.gsfc.nasa .gov/data. Each image represents the Sun seen using many different types of light. Try to make as many of them as you can!

The Science Behind the Fun

Chinese astronomers observed sunspots as early as the year 28 BCE, and Galileo and astronomer Thomas Harriot were the first to observe sunspots using a telescope. A story that is often written about Galileo was that he went blind by observing the Sun. Not true! Galileo did observe the Sun, but he did it by looking at the Sun only at sunrise or sunset or by projecting an image of the Sun onto a wall, not by looking through the telescope at the Sun. If he had looked at the Sun through his telescope, it would have burned his eye pretty much instantly. Galileo and Harriot sketched the spots they saw in their observations. Galileo did go blind late in life, but this was probably due to eye diseases.

Sunspots are areas of the Sun that are a little cooler than the rest of the Sun's surface. Most of the Sun's surface is a sizzling 10,000°F (5,500°C), but sunspots are a chilly 6,700°F (3,700°C). In images of the Sun, sunspots appear darker because they are cooler. Sunspots can last for days, weeks, or even months, and on average, they are planet-size. The Sun goes through cycles where there are many sunspots, then the numbers of sunspots decrease, and then there are periods of time when there are few—or no—spots at all. This cycle lasts about eleven years, on average. You can see the largest sunspots using your pinhole projector, but many will be too small to see. Get in the habit of checking the website spaceweather.com before you go out to see if sunspots are visible. If you can see some, then try to find them using your pinhole projector. Don't be surprised, though, if there are days, weeks, or months with no sunspots. Our Sun doesn't always have them!

Fig. 1: Set up your notebook pages.

Fig. 2: Point your pinhole projector at the Sun.

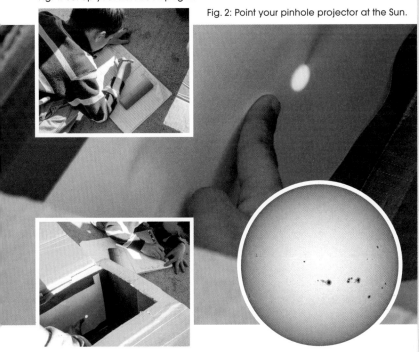

Fig. 3: If you see spots, sketch them in your notebook.

The Sun on July 8, 2014, with several very large sunspots. Most sunspots are smaller than these.

Credit: Solar Dynamics Observatory/ NASA

LAB 45

Our Spinning Sun

Time

10 minutes each day

Materials

- Pinhole projector from Lab 14, "Make a Pinhole Projector" (see page 44)
- Your science notebook
- Pencil
- 1 of the Sun observation pages you made in Lab 44, "Spot Sunspots" (see page 120)

Safety Tips and Setup Hints

- You'll need a fairly sunny day each time you do this lab.
- Do this lab around the time when the Sun is highest in the sky. Always go out at about the same time each day you do this.
- **Never look directly at the Sun**, and do not look through your pinhole or through your pinhole projector at the Sun! Doing so may *very quickly* cause eye damage or blindness.
- You may need someone else with you to hold your pinhole projector in place while you observe the image of the Sun.

Use your observations of the Sun to actually see it spin!

Instructions

Step 1: On a sunny day, point the pinhole end of the projector at the Sun and look for an image of the Sun on your white screen inside the box. (Fig. 1)

Step 2: Move the box just a little. If you can see small dark spots on the image of the Sun that move along with the Sun's image when you move the box, stop and sketch the spots you see. (Fig. 2)

Step 3: Sketch sunspots from your observations using your projector or from the Spaceweather.com website as many days in a row as you can for about thirty days, as long as spots are visible for at least a few of those days. Keep notes in your notebook, especially the dates of your observations. Look back at your observations after a while. What do you notice? ◆

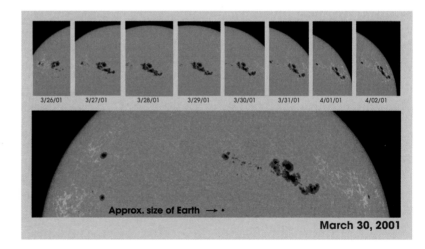

Fig. 1: Point your pinhole projector at the Sun.

Fig. 2: Sketch sunspots as many days in a row as you can.

◀ This set of images was taken by the *SOHO* spacecraft from March 26 through April 2, 2001. Can you see sunspots moving from one side of the Sun to the other?

Credit: Courtesy of SOHO/MDI consortium. SOHO is a project of international cooperation between ESA and NASA.

The Science Behind the Fun

Our Earth spins once every twenty-three hours, fifty-six minutes. Mars's day is a little longer than Earth's day; it spins once every twenty-four hours, thirty-seven minutes. Speedy planet Jupiter rotates once in just nine hours, fifty-five minutes, meaning it spins more than twice before Earth has even spun once. Slowpoke Venus takes 5,832 hours—or the same as 243 Earth *days*—to spin just once.

Our Sun spins, too! Our Sun is made of very hot gas. While we say the Sun has a "surface," it's not a hard surface you can stand on. Different parts of the Sun rotate in different amounts of time. Near the Sun's equator, the hot gas rotates once about every twenty-five Earth days, while the gas near the Sun's north and south poles rotate once about every thirty-six Earth days. We can see the Sun rotate by watching sunspots over time.

Creative Enrichment

Make a flip book out of a set of your Sun sketches or downloaded images of the Sun over several days. Can you see the sunspots move in your pictures?

ORION.

Taurus.

Gemini.

Monoceros.

Cetus.

Eridanus.

Fig. QQ.

Lepus.

Canis Major.

Seeing Stars

People have always looked up at the stars and wondered about them. Stars have been used by adults to teach important lessons to children. Knowing the sky and the ocean allowed very skilled people to travel over the Pacific Ocean thousands of years before GPS. People were connected to the sky, and the stars were a part of everyone's everyday life. Different people around the world were connected to the stars in different ways.

In 1922, astronomers separated the entire sky into eighty-eight constellations, like drawing borders on a map. Each star is a part of only one constellation. The reason they did this was to help scientists tell one another where in the sky they studied different things so all the scientists were using the same set of maps.

Go outside to try to find different groups of stars. It might seem very confusing at first, but if you start with certain stars, such as the Big Dipper or Orion's belt, you can find many others. Give it a try and get to know the sky!

This is a drawing of the constellation Orion the Hunter from the year 1690. This picture shows Orion a little differently from how we see Orion in the real sky. How is it different? Try Lab 49, "Find the Hunter in the Winter" (see page 132), and find out!

Credit: Johannes Hevelius

Find the Dipper and the Pole in Spring

Time

10 minutes

Materials

- Your science notebook
- Pencil

Safety Tips and Setup Hints

- Be careful when you are outside looking at the sky. Make sure you are in a safe location. Wear reflective or light-colored clothing so people can see you.

- If you go out of town to a dark location, have an adult call the nonemergency phone number of the local police to let them know where you are and what you will be doing. Do not set up on private property without the property owner's permission. Follow all local laws. Beware that in many towns, parks close at sunset.

- If you are outside for a long time, you can get cold, even when it isn't that cold. Dress in comfortable layers.

- These instructions work best in May.

To learn your way around the sky, begin with the Big Dipper.

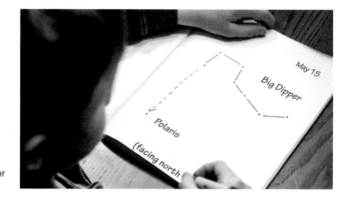

Fig. 2: Sketch the Big Dipper and Polaris.

Instructions

Step 1: Go outside about an hour after sunset in May and face north. If you aren't sure which direction is north, then during the daytime, use Lab 3, "Determining Directions" (see page 18), or use a compass.

Step 2: Look up. The Big Dipper will be hanging "upside down" above you. The bowl of the Big Dipper will be on the left, and the crooked handle will be on the right. Once you find it, sketch it in your notebook. (Fig. 1)

Step 3: Continue to face north. Try to spot the Dipper's crooked handle on the right and the four stars that form the bowl of the Dipper on the left. Look for the two stars on the left side of the bowl. Draw a straight line between those two stars and follow the line down. The next star you run into will be Polaris, the North Star. Make a sketch in your notebook if you found Polaris. (Fig. 2) ✦

Creative Enrichment

There are lots of star maps and constellation books available. If you have a smartphone, get an app that shows you what is in the night sky. Use these resources to plan a family star party! Bring activities for family members to do, make sure everyone dresses in the right clothing, bring bug spray and your science notebook, and don't forget hot chocolate and snacks! Go out as often as you can, and you will start to learn how to find your way around the night sky.

Discover what other people call the Big Dipper. For example, in some parts of the world, the same stars are called the Plow or the Wagon. What else do other people see using those same stars?

The Science Behind the Fun

The Big Dipper is one of the easier groups of stars to find. The shape of the Dipper stars looks like a soup pot with a crooked handle. If you go out to find the Big Dipper, don't worry if you can't see it right away. Finding things in the sky takes practice. The Big Dipper is part of a larger constellation called Ursa Major, the Great Bear. The rest of the stars of the Great Bear are dimmer and harder to see.

Did you notice that Polaris is not very bright? That's because it isn't. There are about forty other stars in the sky that are brighter than the North Star. The reason the North Star is important is that our Earth's North Pole points almost directly at it. As the Earth turns, the stars seem to rise in the east and set in the west, and they appear to turn around the North Star. It looks like it stays in one place. About an hour after sunset in the spring, the Big Dipper will be high up in the north. About an hour after sunset in the summer, the Big Dipper will be in the northwest sky with the bowl pointing down. About an hour after sunset in the fall, the Big Dipper will be low in the sky to the north with the bowl to the right, and about an hour after sunset in the winter, the Big Dipper will be in the northeast sky standing on its handle.

Where you live may change your sky. If you live farther south, things in the sky to the north will be lower. If you live farther north, things in the sky to the north will be higher.

Fig. 1: Look for the Big Dipper in the northern sky.

Find the Triangle in the Summer

Materials
- Your science notebook
- Pencil

Safety Tips and Setup Hints

- Be careful when you are outside looking at the sky. Make sure you are in a safe location. Wear reflective or light-colored clothing so people can see you.

- If you go out of town to a dark location, have an adult call the nonemergency phone number of the local police to let them know where you are and what you will be doing. Do not set up on private property without the property owner's permission. Follow all local laws. Beware that in many towns, parks close at sunset.

- If you are outside for a long time, you can get cold, even when it isn't that cold. Dress in comfortable layers.

- These instructions work best in September.

Three bright stars form a big triangle in the warm summer sky.

Instructions

Step 1: Go outside about two hours after sunset and face south. If you aren't sure which direction is south, then during the daytime, use Lab 3, "Determining Directions" (see page 18), or use a compass. (Fig. 1)

Step 2: Look overhead or nearly overhead. Try to find three bright stars that form a large triangle in the sky. Once you find it, sketch it in your notebook. (Fig. 2)

Step 3: To test your sky skills, try finding the Big Dipper stars from Lab 46, "Find the Dipper and the Pole in Spring" (see page 126). Face north. The Big Dipper will be toward the northwest, or to the left of north. Do you see them? The bowl stars will be on the bottom and the handle will be pointing up.

Step 4: To find another star, look toward the northwest sky and find the Big Dipper. Notice the handle is curved, like part of a circle. Follow the curve away from the bowl toward the south until you see another really bright star. It will have a little bit of an orange color. This is the star called Arcturus (ark-TUR-rus). Make another sketch in your notebook if you can find it. (Fig. 3)

Fig. 1: Go out and look up.

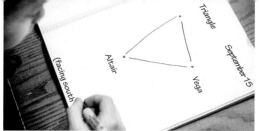

Fig. 2: Sketch the three triangle stars.

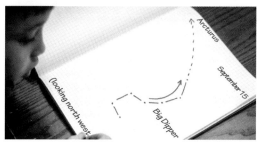

Fig. 3: Follow the arc to Arcturus.

Creative Enrichment

The star name Arcturus comes from an old Greek word, *arktos* (ARK-tohs), which means "bear." The Greek name for Arcturus was Arctouros, which meant "bear watcher" or "bear driver" or "bear guard." Think of that star as keeping an eye on the Great or Big Bear (remember, the Big Dipper stars are part of the Big Bear constellation). Our word *arctic* also comes from this same Greek word for bear. Many of the brightest stars in the sky have interesting names. Find out what different people around the world have used as names for Arcturus, Vega, Altair, and Deneb, and find stories about those star names. Draw pictures to represent some of those stories.

The Science Behind the Fun

As the Earth goes around the Sun, we see different stars depending on the season. The summer sky has lots of bright stars. Face south again. The star in the triangle that is farthest south is called Altair (ALL-tare). The other two stars form the other sides of the triangle, and they are a little farther north than Altair. The one that is on the right, or west, is called Vega (VAY-guh). The star to the left, or east, is called Deneb (DEN-neb). The triangle is made of three stars that are part of three different constellations. Altair is the brightest star in the constellation called Aquila (uh-KWIL-luh) the Eagle. Vega is the brightest star in a small constellation called Lyra (LIE-ruh) the Harp. Deneb is the brightest star in the constellation called Cygnus (SIG-nus) the Swan. The other stars that form those constellations are dimmer, so they can be harder to find, but the triangle can be easier to find since those three stars are bright. This triangle is called the Summer Triangle because it is high in the sky in the summer and early fall after sunset.

A constellation is a group of stars that forms a picture of something, like a connect-the-dots picture. Did you try to find stars that might have looked like a small harp? It's really hard to do, right? If you don't see a harp, or an eagle, or a swan, don't worry. That's because many of the constellations *don't* look much like what they are named for! Lots of people have trouble seeing them. It is much easier to make your own connect-the-dot pictures—which is okay to do!

Find a Flying Horse in the Fall

Time

10 minutes

Materials

- Your science notebook
- Pencil

Safety Tips and Setup Hints

- Be careful when you are outside looking at the sky. Make sure you are in a safe location. Wear reflective or light-colored clothing so people can see you.

- If you go out of town to a dark location, have an adult call the nonemergency phone number of the local police to let them know where you are and what you will be doing. Do not set up on private property without the property owner's permission. Follow all local laws. Beware that in many towns, parks close at sunset.

- If you are outside for a long time, you can get chilled, even when it isn't that cold. Dress in comfortable layers.

- These instructions work best in November.

Horses aren't shaped like squares, right? Well, in the sky, they are!

Instructions

Step 1: Go outside about three hours after sunset and face south. If you aren't sure which direction is south, then during the daytime, use Lab 3, "Determining Directions" (see page 18), or use a compass. (Fig. 1)

Step 2: Look about halfway up in the sky. Try to find four stars in the shape of a large square. Once you find the square, sketch it in your notebook. (Fig. 2)

Step 3: To test your sky skills, try finding the Summer Triangle stars from Lab 47, "Find the Triangle in the Summer" (see page 128). Face west. The three bright stars will be about halfway up in the sky. The one that is highest is Deneb, and Altair and Vega will be below it. Vega will be to the right and Altair will be to the left. (Fig. 3)

Step 4: Now, face north and look for the Big Dipper stars from Lab 46, "Find the Dipper and the Pole in Spring" (see page 126). The Big Dipper will be very low in the sky near the horizon. The bowl will be to the right and the handle will be to the left. Do you see it? (If you live farther south, the Dipper may be below the horizon and not visible.)

Fig. 2: Sketch the square of stars.

Fig. 3: Sketch the triangle and label the stars.

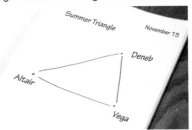

Creative Enrichment

Put on a play to tell the story of Pegasus, Andromeda, and the others. Use props and costumes. Show your play to your family—and get them to join in if you can!

Fig. 1: Go outside and face south.

The Science Behind the Fun

What is this square of stars in the sky? Would you believe it's a flying horse with wings? This is Pegasus (PEG-guh-sus). Some drawings show the square as the body of Pegasus, while others show the square as the horse's wings. There is no wrong way to draw it, though.

There is a story that uses many of the constellations in the sky that you can see in the fall: *Once upon a time*, there was a beautiful girl named Andromeda (an-DRAH-me-duh). Her father was King Cepheus (SEE-fee-us). Her mother was Queen Cassiopeia (cas-see-o-PEH-uh). One day, Queen Cassiopeia was looking at herself in a mirror when she said, aloud, that she was the most beautiful woman in the world. Well, the guardians of the rivers, streams, and seas, called sea nymphs (pronounced NIMFS), heard her. Since *they* thought *they* were the most beautiful women, they got mad and went to Neptune (NEP-toon), the god of the sea. The nymphs asked Neptune to punish Cassiopeia, so Neptune ordered that Princess Andromeda should be chained to a rock by the sea, and she would become lunch for Cetus (SEE-tus) the sea monster. So, Andromeda was chained to a rock. Everyone was at the beach, crying, while they waited for Cetus to arrive. While Cetus swam toward the beach, a little speck appeared in the sky. It got bigger and bigger. It was Perseus (PER-see-us) riding on the back of Pegasus! Cetus came out of the water to grab Andromeda when, all of a sudden, Perseus pulled the head of Medusa (muh-DEW-suh) out of a bag! Cetus saw it and turned instantly to stone! He fell into the water, never to be seen again. Perseus rescued Andromeda, and they all lived *happily ever after*.

LAB 49

Find the Hunter in the Winter

Time

10 minutes

Materials

- Your science notebook
- Pencil

Safety Tips and Setup Hints

- Be careful when you are outside looking at the sky. Make sure you are in a safe location. Wear reflective or light-colored clothing so people can see you.

- If you go out of town to a dark location, have an adult call the nonemergency phone number of the local police to let them know where you are and what you will be doing. Do not set up on private property without the property owner's permission. Follow all local laws. Beware that in many towns, parks close at sunset.

- If you are outside for a long time, you can get chilled, even when it isn't that cold. Dress in comfortable layers.

- These instructions work best in February.

A popular hunter is in the winter sky. If you find his belt, you can find the rest of him!

Instructions

Step 1: Go outside about two hours after sunset and face south. If you aren't sure which direction is south, then during the daytime, use Lab 3, "Determining Directions" (see page 18), or use a compass.

Step 2: Look about halfway up in the sky. Try to find three stars in a row. The star on the left will be a little lower than the star on the right. Once you find it, sketch it in your notebook. (Fig. 1)

Step 3: Look for two stars above the three in a row. They will be bright. The one on the left will be a little more orange in color than the one on the right.

Next, look for two stars below the three in a row. The star on the right will be a little more blue than the star on the left. In all, the three stars in a row, the two stars above, and the two stars below will look like a sideways bow tie. Sketch these stars when you find them. (Fig. 2)

Step 4: To test your sky skills, try finding the square of stars from Lab 48, "Finding a Flying Horse in the Fall" (see page 130). Face west. The square will be on its side pretty low in the western sky. It will look like a square sitting on one of its points. (Fig. 3)

Step 5: Now, face north and look for the Big Dipper stars from Lab 46, "Find the Dipper and the Pole in Spring" (see page 126). The Big Dipper will be in the northeast sky, sitting on its handle with the bowl at the top. ✦

Creative Enrichment

While Orion is the name of this constellation in some parts of the world, it isn't called Orion everywhere. Try to find what other cultures have called the stars of Orion, and make a collage of pictures of what you find.

The Science Behind the Fun

What is this sideways bow tie of stars? This is Orion (o-RIH-un) the Hunter. Many people have heard of Orion, and the stars are bright. The three stars in a row are Orion's belt. The star up and to the left of the belt is an orange-colored star called Betelgeuse (BAY-tel-joos). The star up and to the right of the belt is called Bellatrix (BELL-uh-tricks). Betelgeuse and Bellatrix are Orion's shoulders. The star below and to the left of the belt is Saiph (SIGH-eef), and the star below and to the right of the belt is a blue-white star called Rigel (RIE-jel).

Lots and lots of people on Earth can see the stars that form Orion. In February, it is winter in the Northern Hemisphere and summer in the Southern Hemisphere. At the North Pole in winter, Orion's belt and shoulders go around the horizon, but his knees are below the horizon and can't be seen. The farther south you go, the higher Orion is in the sky. In the United States, Orion is about halfway up in the winter sky. At the equator, Orion rises in the east, goes directly overhead, and sets in the west. If you keep traveling farther south than the equator, it is summertime. Orion would be lower and lower to the north. If you face north, Orion would be standing on his head!

Fig. 1: Sketch the three stars in a row.

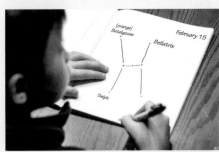

Fig. 2: Sketch the rest of the Hunter's bright stars.

Fig. 3: Go outside and try to find the square horse.

Slide Around the Winter Sky

Time

10 minutes

Materials

- Your science notebook
- Pencil

Safety Tips and Setup Hints

- Be careful when you are outside looking at the sky. Make sure you are in a safe location. Wear reflective or light-colored clothing so people can see you.

- If you go out of town to a dark location, have an adult call the nonemergency phone number of the local police to let them know where you are and what you will be doing. Do not set up on private property without the property owner's permission. Follow all local laws. Beware that in many towns, parks close at sunset.

- If you are outside for a long time, you can get chilled, even when it isn't that cold. Dress in comfortable layers.

- These instructions work best in February.

You can use the stars of Orion to find many others.

Instructions

Step 1: Go outside about two hours after sunset and face south. If you aren't sure which direction is south, then during the daytime, use Lab 3, "Determining Directions" (see page 18), or use a compass. (Fig. 1)

Step 2: Look about halfway up in the sky. Try to find the three stars in a row that form Orion the Hunter's belt. The star on the left will be a little lower than the star on the right. Follow Orion's belt up and to the right. Stop when you get to an orange-colored star. This is the star Aldebaran (al-DEB-uh-rahn). Aldebaran will be part of a small V of stars. This V of stars is a cluster, or group, of stars called the Hyades (HIGH-uh-deez). A little to the right of the V is another small group that looks like a really tiny dipper. This tiny group is called the Pleiades (PLEE-uh-deez), or the Seven Sisters. Sketch these stars in your notebook. (Fig. 2)

Step 3: Go back to Orion's belt stars. Follow the belt down and to the left. Stop when you reach a really bright star. This is the star Sirius (SEER-ree-us). Sketch this star in your notebook. (Fig. 3)

Step 4: Look for the two bright stars above Orion's belt. These are Betelgeuse and Bellatrix. Draw a line between Bellatrix and Betelgeuse and follow it to the left. Stop when you get to another bright star. This is the star Procyon (PRO-see-on). If you connect Procyon, Betelgeuse, and Sirius, you should see a triangle, with Procyon and Betelgeuse at the top, and Sirius at the bottom. These three stars are also called the Winter Triangle. Sketch these stars in your notebook. (Fig. 4)

Fig. 1: Go outside and find the Dipper.

Fig. 2: Sketch the small V and the tiny "dipper."

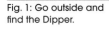
Fig. 3: Sketch Sirius.

Fig. 4: Sketch the bright triangle.

Creative Enrichment

The Pleiades are often called the Seven Sisters. For centuries, people used the Pleiades to test eyesight. Most people can see four to six stars. Some with really good eyesight can see eight to ten stars. With extremely good eyesight, some people can see thirteen or fourteen stars. Try to see how many you can find when you are out under a really dark sky. Sketch the ones you can see and compare your sketch to a picture of the Pleiades. How did you do? Another eyesight test is the star that is in the bend in the handle of the Big Dipper. This is the star Mizar (MY-zahr). There is a dim star really close to it. This star's name is Alcor (AL-cohr). Can you see Alcor?

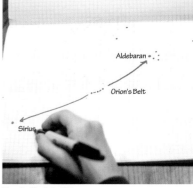

The Science Behind the Fun

By finding one group of stars, you can find many more in the sky. This is a great way to start to learn where things are! Did you notice some stars had a little color? Look at orange-colored Betelgeuse and Aldebaran. Look at white-colored Sirius. The color actually means something. Star color tells you star temperature. Red and orange stars are the coolest, yellow and white stars are medium temperature, and blue-white and blue stars are the hottest. Now, these colors are not bright colors, so don't expect to see Betelgeuse looking like a bright red stop sign, but you can see a little bit of color. Are these colors surprising to you? We're used to using blue to represent cold and red to represent hot, but star colors are the opposite. Red means cool and blue means hot.

Aldebaran is the brightest star in the constellation of Taurus (TOR-us) the Bull. Sirius, the brightest star in our nighttime sky, is part of the constellation of Canis (CANE-nuhs) Major, the Big Dog. Procyon is part of the constellation of Canis Minor, the Little Dog.

See the Lion and the Queen in Spring

Time

10 minutes

Materials

- Your science notebook
- Pencil

Safety Tips and Setup Hints

- Be careful when you are outside looking at the sky. Make sure you are in a safe location. Wear reflective or light-colored clothing so people can see you.

- If you go out of town to a dark location, have an adult call the nonemergency phone number of the local police to let them know where you are and what you will be doing. Do not set up on private property without the property owner's permission. Follow all local laws. Beware that in many towns, parks close at sunset.

- If you are outside for a long time, you can get chilled, even when it isn't that cold. Dress in comfortable layers.

- These instructions work best in May.

Our Big Dipper can help us find even more star groups.

Instructions

Step 1: Go outside about an hour after sunset in May and face north. If you aren't sure which direction is north, then during the daytime, use Lab 3, "Determining Directions" (see page 18), or use a compass.

Step 2: Look up. The Big Dipper will be hanging "upside down" above you. The bowl of the Big Dipper will be on the left, and the crooked handle will be on the right. Now, turn around and face south. Look overhead. Now, the Big Dipper's bowl will be on the right and the handle will be on the left. Once you find it, sketch it in your notebook. (Fig. 1)

Step 3: Now, keep facing south. Imagine the bowl of the Big Dipper is filled with water. Poke a hole in the Dipper's bowl, and all the water falls out through the hole onto more stars. The right side of the group looks like a backward question mark—ʕ—and the left side looks like a small triangle. The backward question mark is the head and neck of Leo the Lion. The small triangle is Leo's back legs and tail. Once you find Leo, sketch him in your notebook. (Fig. 2)

Step 4: Next, turn around and face north again. Look for the Big Dipper. Draw a line through the two stars farthest from the handle to Polaris, the North Star. Keep going down and a little to the left until you see a W of stars. The W might be a bit sideways, so it could look a bit like this: Σ. This W is Cassiopeia the Queen. Make a sketch of Cassiopeia in your notebook. (If you live farther south, the Queen may be below the horizon and not visible.) (Fig. 3)

Creative Enrichment

Try to make your own planetarium. There are many ways to do it—but make sure an adult is there to help. Use constellation books or pictures online to choose your stars. Grab some paper cups and poke holes in the bottom to represent different constellations. Put a flashlight into the cup and shine the "stars" on the ceiling. Or, to make a bigger planetarium, use a large oatmeal container and a bright LED light or large flashlight. There are also directions and videos online to make your own planetarium dome! You can also make constellations using glow-in-the-dark stars or strings of holiday lights. Use your imagination to bring the night sky indoors!

The Science Behind the Fun

The Big Dipper can be a useful group of stars! Follow the two bowl stars to the North Star. Keep going to Cassiopeia. Follow the curve of the handle to Arcturus. Let the water in the bowl fall onto Leo the Lion. As long as you can find that Dipper, you have a good chance to find more!

As you learned in Lab 46, "Find the Dipper and the Pole in Spring" (see page 126), our Earth's North Pole points almost right at Polaris. As the Earth turns, everything seems to turn around the North Star. Now, depending on where you live, you may notice some of the stars right around that Pole star never set. The farther north you go, Polaris is higher and higher in the sky and more stars in the sky never seem to set. When you are right at the North Pole, all the stars seem to turn around Polaris and none of them set. The farther south you go, Polaris is lower and lower, and fewer stars around Polaris never set. Right at the Earth's equator, all the stars rise and set. If you keep going south, you can't see Polaris anymore because it is below the horizon. You may wonder if the Earth's South Pole points to a "South Star." No, there is no South Star. The fact that we have a star in the spot where the North Pole points is just by chance. If you are south of the equator and you want to try to find where the South Pole points, some people use a constellation called the Southern Cross. The bottom of the cross points toward where the south sky pole would be, a little farther away.

Fig. 1: Go outside and find the Dipper.

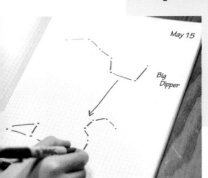

Fig. 2: Sketch the Lion's stars.

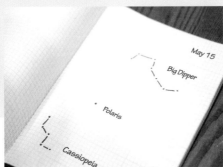

Fig. 3: Draw the Queen's W.

Supernova Bounce

Time

5 minutes

Materials

- Tennis ball
- Soccer ball or basketball

Safety Tips and Setup Hints

- Do this lab outside on a hard surface. Don't do this near windows or anything breakable.

Fig. 1: Hold a tennis ball out and then drop it.

Fig. 2: Hold a soccer ball or basketball out and then drop it.

One of Orion's stars will "go supernova" someday. What does this mean?

Fig. 3: Drop the tennis ball and soccer ball or basketball together.

Instructions

Step 1: Hold the tennis ball out at arm's length in front of you. Predict how high the ball will bounce when you let go and drop it. Drop the ball and observe how high it bounces. (Fig. 1)

Step 2: Hold the soccer ball or basketball out at arm's length in front of you. Predict how high the ball will bounce when you let go and drop it. Drop the ball and observe how high it bounces. (Fig. 2)

Step 3: Hold the tennis ball on top of the soccer ball or basketball so they touch. Predict how high the two balls will bounce when you drop them together. Drop the two balls together and observe how high they bounce. How did this compare to dropping them one by one? (Fig. 3) ✦

Creative Enrichment

Make star-color cookies, and make sure an adult is there to help if you need it. Grab your favorite sugar cookie dough. Roll out your dough and cut out round cookies—because stars are round! Follow the recipe and bake your cookies. After they have cooled, make white icing or frosting. Leave some of it white, but use food coloring to tint the icing red, orange, yellow, blue-white, and blue. Ice or frost your cookies to represent all the different colors of stars. If you let the icing dry, you can even use a tube of dark blue or black icing gel to write the names of stars on the right color cookies. Enjoy your cookie stars!

The Science Behind the Fun

Stars make energy in their centers. This center is called the star's "core." Making energy is what makes a star a "star."

Stars are made of a lot of material, and this causes the star to have a huge pull of gravity. Really large stars have a huge amount of mass. Gravity wants to pull all the star's hot gas together, while the energy from the core pushes the hot gas out. What would happen if a really large star stopped making energy? There would be no energy pushing out. Gravity pulls the outer parts of the star in, and a little of the hot gas explodes outward. This is a supernova.

When you dropped the soccer ball or basketball together with the tennis ball, the tennis ball absorbed the energy of the soccer ball or basketball, so the tennis ball bounced much higher.

In this lab, think of the star like layers of an onion. The ground under your feet represents the densest part of the center of the star. The soccer ball or basketball represents the outer layers of the center of the star, and the tennis ball represents the outer layers of the rest of the star. When a supernova happens, most of the mass of the star stays with the core, just like most of the mass in this lab was the ground below your feet. Only a small amount of the star explodes outward, which is represented by the tennis ball.

Will a supernova happen to our Sun? No. Supernovas only happen to stars a lot larger than our Sun. If you looked for the stars of Orion the Hunter in Lab 49, "Find the Hunter in the Winter" (see page 132), you spotted a star that will explode sometime in the next million years or so: Betelgeuse. When this happens, Betelgeuse will look really bright in the sky for a while, and then it will fade away. Orion will no longer have two shoulders!

More Resources

Do you want to continue the astronomy fun? Many resources are in your town or online. Here are some suggestions:

- The best way to learn the sky is to keep trying! Go out as often as you can, and keep observing, sketching, and taking notes. Watch the Moon during the day and at night. Watch the constellations from month to month. Look for sunrise and sunset. Try to get out to a dark sky spot when you can. Look back at your notes from time to time and see how much you have learned. Do this before you buy a telescope. It can be easier to use a telescope when you first know what you are looking at.

- Visit your local planetarium or science museum. Many of them have programs to show you what is in tonight's night sky, and this program changes all year long as the seasons change and you can see different stars. Some of them also have night sky telescope programs.

- Visiting a planetarium might be a good idea to do before you try Labs 46 through 51 (see pages 126 through 136). It's also a good idea if you want to learn how to find Mercury, Venus, Mars, Jupiter, or Saturn in the night sky. Earth moves and these planets move, so they are not in the same part of the sky every year and they can be harder to learn.

- Find out if your local planetarium or science museum offers camp or overnight programs, or find out what age you need to be to volunteer there.

- Find a local astronomy club. Many of them have programs that anyone can go to, and the members may even set up telescopes after the meeting. Other clubs set up telescopes in public locations. Walk up and take a look!

- Look for astronomy podcasts online or in an app store.

- Some local libraries have telescopes or binoculars you can check out for a few weeks. Try before you buy!

- Look for stargazing or "star party" activities at parks, museums, and planetariums. Many times, these events happen when there are interesting things happening in the sky, such as eclipses or meteor showers.

- There are many ways you can help do real science! Search for "citizen science" programs online, such as:
  - Zooniverse: www.zooniverse.org
  - NASA S'COOL Rover Cloud Observations program: scool.larc.nasa.gov

- Want to know what is going on in the Universe? Check out NASA's website, www.nasa.gov, or the European Space Agency's website, www.esa.int.

- If you need to find out your local time for sunrise, sunset, moonrise, and moonset, or if you need to find out Moon phases, go to the U.S. Naval Observatory's website: aa.usno.navy.mil.

- There are many different space telescopes that NASA has to look at nearby and faraway things in the Universe:
  - Spitzer Space Telescope: www.spitzer.caltech.edu
  - Hubble Space Telescope: www.hubblesite.org
  - Chandra X-Ray Observatory: chandra.harvard.edu
  - Fermi Gamma-ray Space Telescope: fermi.gsfc.nasa.gov

- Want to learn more about Mars? Visit mars.jpl.nasa.gov.

- Download and use free computer planetarium software, such as:
  - Stellarium: www.stellarium.org
  - WorldWide Telescope: www.worldwidetelescope.org

- You can take your own pictures of things in the night sky using MicroObservatory: www.cfa.harvard.edu/smg/website/own.

- There is something interesting in the sky every night. Find out where to look at www.earthsky.org/tonight.

Thank You!

Matthew

Kathryn

Darwin

Novella

Madison

Claudia

Mikayla

Arlo

Analise

Ruby

Logan

Elio

Elijah

Acknowledgments

So many people have assisted me with this book and I would like to acknowledge them here, though my thanks will never be enough in return for all the help they gave me. First and foremost, thank you to my husband, Brian, who encouraged me throughout this entire process, and thanks to my entire family.

Thanks are due to all the staff at Quarry Books and all the editors and designers for their patience, kindness, and enthusiasm. Jonathan Simcosky, you and your fellow staff took a chance on a rookie author, and for that, I am grateful.

I must acknowledge the beautiful work of my photographer, David Miller. You made these activities shine like no one else could.

Thank you to all the moms and dads (most especially Kelli Landes, Joe Kim, and Glenn and Barb Yehling) who agreed to allow their children to appear in photos for this book—and a huge thanks to the kids, too!

Finally, thank you to all of the hundreds of staff, past and present, I have worked with at the Adler Planetarium. You all have inspired me to be a better educator.

I hope this book makes all of you proud!

About the Author

Michelle Nichols is Master Educator at the Adler Planetarium in Chicago, Illinois, where she has worked for more than twenty years. She earned a bachelor of science degree from the University of Illinois at Urbana-Champaign and a master of education degree from National-Louis University. Michelle is an avid night sky watcher, and she also loves to run, cook, garden, and cheer on her favorite Chicago sports teams. She lives in the suburbs of Chicago with her husband.

Index